Time Management for New Employees

Unlock the secrets of effective time management with strategies and tools designed to boost your productivity

Prakash V. Rao

Impackt Publishing
We Mean Business

Time Management for New Employees

Copyright © 2015 Impackt Publishing

All rights reserved. No part of this book may be reproduced, stored in a retrieval system, or transmitted in any form or by any means, without the prior written permission of the publisher, except in the case of brief quotations embedded in critical articles or reviews.

Every effort has been made in the preparation of this book to ensure the accuracy of the information presented. However, the information contained in this book is sold without warranty, either express or implied. Neither the author, nor Impackt Publishing, and its dealers and distributors will be held liable for any damages caused or alleged to be caused directly or indirectly by this book.

Impackt Publishing has endeavored to provide trademark information about all of the companies and products mentioned in this book by the appropriate use of capitals. However, Impackt Publishing cannot guarantee the accuracy of this information.

First published: April 2015

Production reference: 1270415

Published by Impackt Publishing Ltd.
Livery Place
35 Livery Street
Birmingham B3 2PB, UK.

ISBN 978-1-78300-052-4

www.Impacktpub.com

Credits

Author
Prakash V. Rao

Reviewers
Aung Ko Ko
Keshav Kumar

Acquisition Editor
Richard Gall

Content Development Editor
Sweny Sukumaran

Copy Editor
Sharvari H. Baet

Project Coordinators
Priyanka Goel
Rashi Khivansara

Proofreaders
Simran Bhogal
Maria Gould
Paul Hindle

Graphics
Sheetal Aute
Disha Haria
Abhinash Sahu
Skanda Rao

Production Coordinator
Melwyn D'sa

Cover Work
Simon Cardew

About the Author

Prakash V. Rao is trained in computer engineering and management with master's degrees in both fields. With about 30 years of experience in the corporate world, he has risen from the cubicle trenches through the ranks of management up to director and vice-president for two multi-billion-dollar corporations before starting his management consulting practice. As a consultant, Prakash focuses on the areas of management tactics and productivity, and towards this latter end, he has developed several techniques to improve effectiveness, efficiency, and time management. He is now a recognized expert in the area of time management, having authored a book and several articles, having been interviewed on radio and television, and having conducted over 1000 lectures, workshops, and seminars.

Prakash's company, Bank Your Time, provides classroom training, seminars, and workshops in time management and productivity. His courses are also available online as webinars and e-learning content.

Prakash's original approach to teaching time management, the Bank Your Time game, has been adopted by over 1000 users. The details of this game are available in his book, *The Bank Your Time Game: Rulebook and Play Guide*, ETA publishing.

This book is dedicated to my family—my wife, Bhavani, and our boys, Ananth and Skanda—whose love and support fuels me on to greater heights. Moreover, my older son Ananth was my first ever student in time management—in teaching him, I was inspired to enter the field of time management training and spread the message to others—and my younger boy Skanda was the artist who created some of the images in this book. The book could not have been created without editorial support initially from Richard Gall and then from Sweny Sukumaran, nor could it have come to light without Priyanka Goel's persistence and coordination.

About the Reviewers

Aung Ko Ko is a doctor who turned to management. Having grown up inspired by characters from video games and cartoons, he incorporates the most unconventional of training methods in the sessions he designs and delivers. He was awarded the Top Paper Prize for Human Resource Management by The Association of Business Executives, United Kingdom (ABE, UK), in June 2012, and is currently working his way to a master's degree in human resources management.

Contents

Preface	**1**
Chapter 1: What is Time Management?	**13**
The limited view and the big picture	13
Signs and results of poor time management	15
Benefits of time management	17
A definition of time management	18
Activity management	19
Event control	19
Dividing the pies	20
Exercise	22
Discussion and illustration	23
Summary	24
Chapter 2: Setting Goals	**25**
Values	25
Value system	26
Benefit	28
Exercise	28
Goals	29
Benefit	31
SMART goals	32
Benefits of having SMART goals	32
Exercise	33
Action plans	34
Short-term objectives	34
Daily activities	36
Exercise	37
Summary	37
Chapter 3: Task Management	**39**
Activity lists	40
The to-do list	41

Exercises	42
Prioritization	42
The A-1 method	43
Importance and urgency	43
Exercises	45
Filtering tasks	45
The 4 Ds	45
The Pareto Principle	47
Exercises	48
Task dependencies	48
Exercise	49
Summary	49

Chapter 4: Schedule Management — 51

Definitions	52
Exercise	53
Handling appointments	53
Maintaining appointments	54
Preparing for an appointment	54
The appointment	55
Follow-up	56
Exercise	56
Meetings	56
Agenda	56
Agenda item resolution	57
Meeting minutes	58
Exercises	58
Summary	59

Chapter 5: Managing Daily Tasks — 61

Managing expectations	61
Unrealistic expectations	62
Dealing with expectations efficiently	65
Exercise	66
Estimation	67
Creating a realistic daily tasks list	70
Exercise	72
Summary	72

Chapter 6: Deadline Management — 73

Parkinson's Law	73
Murphy's Law	76
Student's Syndrome	78
Strategies	79
Strategy 1 – Frontend load	79

Strategy 2 – Artificial deadlines	83
Strategy 3 – Failure management	84
Summary	85

Chapter 7: Overcoming Obstacles to Productivity — 87

Obstacles	87
Internal obstacles	88
Professional obstacles	89
Emotion	90
Thought issues	91
Action issues	92
Preparation	93
Crisis management	95
Interruption management	96
Self-discipline	97
Taking responsibility	98
Deliberate distractions	99
Exercises	100
Summary	100

Chapter 8: Measuring Your Time Management Skills — 101

Why measure?	101
What should be measured?	102
Collecting metrics	104
Using the metrics	105
How to be more productive	106
How to be more effective	106
How to be more efficient	107
How to be more punctual	108
How to be more dependable	108
How to improve quality	109
Summary	109

Chapter 9: Tools — 111

Tasks	111
The process for managing tasks	112
Appointments and meetings	113
Paper products	113
Day-Timer	114
Franklin Covey planner	115
Technology	116
Outlook calendar	116
Google calendar	117
The process for managing appointments	117
Deadlines	118
The process for managing deadlines	118
Summary	119

› Preface

A person is hired for his/her skills, abilities, experience, attitude, and other promising factors, but the person is rewarded for performance—or fired for the lack of it. Time management is a critical skill that helps deliver promised performance. Time management is a practical skill and, therefore, any training program, workshop, seminar, or book addressing this skill must use a hands-on approach. This is a practical book. It is not meant to be merely read but to be applied and practiced. This preface states the objective of the course and lays out the manner in which the objective may be met, that is, the target behavior and the methodology by which the target behavior may be instilled.

Behavior and change

Around 350 BC, Aristotle stated his concepts of Physics, the general principles of change that govern all natural bodies, both living and inanimate. One of his concepts was that heavier objects fell to the earth faster than lighter bodies. In 1589, Galileo dropped two balls of different masses from the Leaning Tower of Pisa to prove that the fall of bodies is independent of their mass. Yet, for over a hundred years more, the University of Pisa still taught their students the Aristotelian version of the principle.

Galileo stated and proved his concept. He did not change beliefs. He did not change behavior patterns.

During the initial years of my corporate career, I took several time management courses and read many more books on the subject. Nothing worked for me until I discovered the true reason why nothing worked for me: merely carrying around an organizer/planner, noting appointments and tasks in it, and hoping for the best does not constitute time management. Unless I changed my behavior, I could only get the same old results. Einstein defined insanity as "Doing the same thing over and over again and expecting different results." I realize now that my behavior at that time could have well been classified as insanity by Einstein's definition.

Time management is not a skill—it is a pattern of thought and behavior based on beliefs, attitudes, intentions, and commitment. Time management training goes beyond stating facts and proving concepts. It involves changing attitudes and behavior patterns.

What changes behavior? Behavior can only be changed through strong motivation that emerges from dissatisfaction with the current state and a deep desire to reach a better state.

This book is intended to help the reader acquire the appropriate beliefs, attitudes, intentions, and commitments required for time management and to bring about the required change in behavior.

A brief history of time management

There have been references to proper use of time in all ancient texts and philosophies. Roman Senator and Philosopher Marcus Aurelius (121-180 CE) said, "Remember that man's life lies all within this present, as 't were but a hair's-breadth of time; as for the rest, the past is gone, the future yet unseen."

Benjamin Franklin is considered the father of time management. He eschewed wasting even a moment. His writings have several references to time management. His posthumous autobiography shows his system for the pursuit of "Order." In a small book of his own making, he assiduously tracked each day's activities.

Modern time management dates back to the 1910 classic *How to Live on 24 Hours a Day* by Arnold Bennett. In this, Bennett urges salaried workers to claim extra time and use the extra time to improve themselves and to really live as opposed to merely existing.

US President Dwight D. Eisenhower said, "The more important an item, the less likely it is urgent, and the more urgent an item, the less likely it is important." He used an importance/urgency matrix to classify tasks and identify the one(s) that required immediate attention.

In 1973, Alan Lakein brought forth his classic, *How to Get Control of Your Time and Your Life*. He is credited as the creator of *Lakein's Question*, "What is the best use of my time right now?" His A-1 technique is still the most powerful prioritization technique for ensuring that time is effectively used.

Hyrum W. Smith founded the Franklin Quest Company in 1981 and created the Franklin Planner. In 1997, he merged his company with Stephen Covey's Covey Leadership Center to form Franklin Covey, one of the world's leading providers of time management training and planner/organizer products.

David Allen brought his perspectives on productivity to Lockheed in the 1980s and went on to create a time management program called *Getting Things Done* in 2001.

In 2002, yours truly, the author of the book that you hold in your hand, created a game called *Bank Your Time* to teach time management to teens and youths. The game became a popular time-management training program in several corporations. What you hold in your hand combines traditional time management concepts with ideas from the Bank Your Time game.

Indirection and control

Let me introduce you to the concept of "indirection." There are several ways of getting a task done:

- Do it yourself
- Delegate someone else to do it
- Forbid your children from doing it!

Levity aside, when you delegate a task to someone else, you are creating a level of indirection, that is, you get the results not from direct action but from indirect action. Now, if that someone further delegates the task, there is another level of indirection created. With each delegation or level of indirection, you get farther removed from the ultimate action and you have less control over the process. How do you ensure that the task is completed to your standards? The solution is to give up control and grant power (empowerment) while stressing the benefits of the action and the value it provides.

Why am I belaboring this point?

Let us take the subject of teaching. When I teach the material covered in this book, I have control over the process. I impart knowledge (content) through instruction presentation, examples, analogies, stories, activities, and exercises. With this Workshop in a Box, I delegate the teaching to you and introduce a level of indirection. I grant you control over the process. How can I influence the way that you teach?

I could put on my professorial face and pontificate as to what you MUST do in order to teach this material. Rather than that, allow me to advise you. Let me share with you my knowledge, experiences in teaching this material, the stories and illustrations I use to get the point across, and the activities and exercises that I use to drill the students in the concepts. In short, let me share with you my content, my lesson plans, and my teaching methodology.

The strength of this book is that it exists at two levels—concepts and teaching aids. At the first level, I give you material for you to use in training your students. At the second level, I show you how I train my students so that you may use the same approach in your workshops.

What is the process of effective teaching? How does one learn a skill? Can one learn to play soccer by merely reading a book or attending a workshop? While the intellectual aspects of the skill—the concepts—may get absorbed into the conscious part of the mind from a book or a workshop, it will not become integrated into the person's behavior except by application.

In the old view of education, the teacher was the active participant and the student a passive participant in a process that broadcast knowledge. In the current view of education, both the teacher and the student are active participants in a partnership that transfers knowledge. In other words, in the old world, teaching was done to the student. In the new world, learning is done by the student. Therefore, I begin every one of my workshops by introducing the students to the concept of active learning and teaching them how to learn. The ability to learn is very useful. The students can then go on to quickly absorb other skills from other teachers. Indeed, this is the first benefit my students receive even before they learn the actual skills contained in my workshop.

In the following section, do note that I am indifferent as to the subject or discipline that I am teaching and helping my students learn. I use the same methodology in all my workshops, be it a workshop on time management, problem solving and decision making, project management or management tactics.

How to use this book

How does one learn a skill? Can one learn to play soccer by merely reading a book or attending a workshop? While the intellectual aspects of the skill—the concepts—may get absorbed into the conscious part of the mind from a book or a workshop, it will not become integrated into the person's behavior except by application.

There is a five-stage process for effective learning. The concepts in this book are presented in such a manner as to move the reader along the five stages and acquire this skill. The stages are: preparation, presentation, processing, padding, and propping.

> **Stage 1: Preparation**
>
> In this stage, the individual's mind is prepared to receive the concept and skill. This stage has three activities:
>
> > **Motivation**
> >
> > Why should you acquire this knowledge, skill, or habit? What is in it for you? The human mind is much enamored by the WIIFM (What's In It For Me) factor. When an individual knows the benefits, their mind is eager to acquire the skill and reap the benefits. Motivation overcomes barriers to learning such as resistance to change and the fear of stepping outside the comfort zone.
> >
> > **Positive mental attitude**
> >
> > It is said that if you think that you *can* do something or if you think that you *cannot* do the same thing, you are right. It is the belief that you have in yourself that helps you achieve—or not achieve—whatever you set out to do. Even if the reader has the motivation, if they do not have the faith that they are capable of learning a concept or skill, no amount of effort will enable them to learn. It is important to be confident in one's ability to learn. A positive mental attitude overcomes barriers to learning such as doubt ("I am not smart enough to learn this", "This is too complex", "I don't have the background for this material.")

- **Receptive state**

    After motivating the individual and creating the positive mental attitude, it is important to put them in a receptive state. You must be relaxed, ready, confident, and eager to learn. The two techniques I use for this are meditation and positive affirmations. A receptive state overcomes barriers to learning such as self-sabotage.

Stage 2: Presentation

I have seen the following words on a poster on a teacher's wall:

"Tell me and I will forget.

Show me and I may remember.

Involve me and I will understand."

How can you involve everyone? What captivates and captures attention such that teaching is almost automatic? There are four general attention grabbers:

- **Stories**

    Never underestimate the power of a story. Aesop's Fables have been used to instruct children in values and morals for millennia. Plato's Dialogues show that Socrates used this technique to teach philosophy. The Bible and other religious texts contain many stories that communicate certain truths about the religion gently and subtly. Bruce Barton, American marketing legend, set out all his marketing messages as parables. Shakespeare said that a picture is worth a thousand words. This is true of static pictures that only require words of static description. However, words that tell a story paint dynamic pictures in the mind. These require action words and dynamic descriptions. Such stories are often worth a thousand pictures.

- **Games**

    How did you learn as a child and toddler? How do children in pre-school, kindergarten, and Montessori schools learn? Games are an essential part of early learning but are largely ignored in later education. I introduce some concepts through games, role-playing, and enactment.

- **Challenges**

    The human cannot resist challenges, more so when some rewards are promised to the winner. I often divide the participants into groups and play them against each other to meet some targets (the first to enumerate all benefits of ..., the first to demonstrate ...) and award the group with the highest score the promised reward.

- **Arguments**

    It is said that you learn best when you teach someone else or when you defend a position or point of view. I pick some students and play the devil's advocate. In convincing me that I am wrong, the students learn the concept.

Another aspect of presentation is that people use different learning styles. Some are visual learners, some auditory, some tactile/kinesthetic, and very few are olfactory or gustatory. It is necessary to present the same concept in different modes so as to fit all learning styles. You cannot show an auditory learner, nor have a tactile/kinesthetic learner listen to something. Using multiple modes of presentation also serves to reinforce the concept.

➤ Stage 3: Processing

In the Bloom's *Taxonomy of Cognitive Learning*, Benjamin Bloom defined six stages in the process of learning:

- ➢ **Acquiring information and remembering**, wherein the student merely memorizes the concepts without really understanding.
- ➢ **Paraphrasing**, wherein by stating the concept in his/her own words, the student begins to understand the concept.
- ➢ **Applying**, wherein the student puts the concept to practical use and relates it to real world context.
- ➢ **Analysis**, wherein the student breaks down the concept into constituent parts, makes inferences and finds generalizations.
- ➢ **Synthesis**, wherein the student combines the concept with prior knowledge and skills to rearrange, adapt, formulate, and create extensions to the concept.
- ➢ **Evaluation**, wherein the student judges the value of the materials and critiques and supports and reframes the knowledge.

In my workshop, I encourage the students to follow the taxonomy by paraphrasing, relating to real-world examples (application), and moving on to analysis, synthesis, and evaluation. The last, evaluation, is the most important: by assigning value to the concept and relating it to the motivation, the circle is complete and the purpose of the learning is established. For example, in this workshop, many of my classroom exercises involve discussions to analyze and evaluate the concepts covered.

➤ Stage 4: Padding

We all have different experiences, and relate differently to the same information. A friend of mine stated it very succinctly, "We don't see things as they are; we see things as we are." Therefore, even with the foregoing steps and learning, students will have gaps in their understanding according to their experiences. Prerequisite knowledge forms the basis or platform of understanding upon which new concepts can be built. This includes enough information such that there is no misunderstanding or miscommunication. It allows new concepts to be linked and anchored to the platform through associations.

The human brain is a pattern making and pattern recognizing system. It builds the patterns through associations. Incomplete information or lack of some prerequisite knowledge reduces some of the associations, which may lead to bias, prejudice, or dogma.

As Alexander Pope wrote:

"A little knowledge is a dangerous thing;

Drink deep, or taste not the Pierian spring

where shallow draughts intoxicate the brain

and drinking largely sobers us again"

After the presentation phase, it is useful to explore how well a student has understood the concept, to identify gaps in understanding, and pad the gaps so as to complete the picture. Padding is the process where the gaps in understanding are closed.

> **Stage 5: Propping**

When a young tree is transplanted, stakes are driven into the ground next to the tree and lines are securely tied from the stakes to the tree. These stakes remain in place until the tree takes root and is able to stand on its own. Similarly, new concepts are anchored to existing concepts with associative links such that the power of association holds the new concept in place until it takes root. Association is a very powerful way to learn new concepts.

Propping or association is a very powerful way of creating new habits. By always linking one action to another such that one automatically triggers the other, behavior patterns are created and strongly established. Therefore, in order to take on a new habit it can be anchored to an existing habit through forced links. This was the mechanism used by the great Russian psychologist Ivan Pavlov used to create conditioned reflexes. His famous experiment with the dog and the bell wherein he rang the bell each time he fed the dog such that just by ringing the bell he caused the dog to salivate speaks for this mechanism of association as a way to change behavior.

What this book covers

The book is laid out in nine chapters as described below.

Chapter 1, What is Time Management?, sets the stage for the rest of the workshop. The term *time management* means different things to different people. This chapter lays a common frame of understanding by exploring what people believe about time management, enumerating the benefits of time management, formally defining the term time management, briefly going over the history of time management, and showing how time management can lead to success.

Chapter 2, *Setting Goals*, sets a clear direction by establishing values, visions, and goals. When values, visions, goals, and actions are congruent, the results will be in line with expectations.

Chapter 3, *Task Management*, is the cornerstone of time management. Earl Nightingale said that time cannot be managed except through the control of activities. This chapter shows how activities can be managed by making lists, prioritizing, and pruning. This chapter also shows how dependent actions and sequences of actions can be managed together.

Chapter 4, *Schedule Management*, shows how to use planners and organizers. Schedule management is another key concept in time management. It promotes punctuality. Schedule management involves keeping track of appointments, meetings, and deadlines in a daily planner and to set yourself reminders to meet these expectations. A reputation for punctuality leads to a reputation for responsibility, reliability, and accountability.

Chapter 5, *Managing Daily Tasks*, shows how to manage the day's activities. It is important to know how much time is available and how long any task will take in order to make a realistic list of tasks for the day. This sets achievable expectations.

Chapter 6, *Deadline Management*, focuses on getting things done on time. It is the complementary concept to schedule management. While schedule management ensures that you be somewhere at a given time, deadline management ensures that you do something by a given time. Deadline management addresses issues and obstacles that prevent on-time completion of tasks. These issues include Parkinson's Law, procrastination, Murphy's Law, and risks.

Chapter 7, *Overcoming Obstacles to Productivity*, covers tactics to get work done quickly and with fewest errors. This includes dealing with interruptions and distractions. It also covers areas of self-discipline such as preparation, organization, delegation, and accepting responsibility.

Chapter 8, *Measuring Your Time Management Skills*, shows how to measure the effectiveness of time management. It is said that if you cannot measure it you cannot manage it. The metrics covered in this chapter show productivity, effectiveness, efficiency, and quality. Metrics boost self image and allow you to take pride in your achievements.

Chapter 9, *Tools*, introduces tools that may be used to implement time management concepts and actions, including calendars, to-do lists, reminders, and alarms.

Make a note

Each concept in every chapter going forward is laid out in the following manner:

- Concept definition
- Benefit, that is, value or motivation
- Prerequisite knowledge, if any
- Presentation materials, for example, stories, analogies, games, and so on
- Application of the concept, that is, how it relates to the real world
- Associations
- Exercises

Each concept can be independently learned and linked or associated to previous concepts.

This is an action-oriented book. Its purpose is to influence behavior and produce results. While some theory and history where relevant are given, actions are the biggest takeaways.

The proof of the pudding is in the eating. The proof of this book is in the improved productivity that will be seen in every individual touched directly or indirectly by this book.

Who this book is for

Most, if not all, businesses rate time management as one of the most important skills in their employees. Good time management leads to better productivity and profitability. Training in time management will enable businesses be more efficient and effective. This book is targeted at three groups of individuals. It is designed to bring a new employee up to speed in time management. It will also help managers guide their teams, especially new hires, in time management just as a master craftsman guides apprentices. Finally, it will serve as reference material for trainers and coaches who offer time management courses.

Conventions

In this book, you will find a number of styles of text that distinguish between different kinds of information. Here are some examples of these styles, and an explanation of their meaning.

New terms and **important words** are shown in bold.

📗	**For Reference** For Reference appear like this

📋	**Lists** Lists appear like this

➡	**Action Point** Action points appear like this

✏	**Make a note** Warnings or important notes appear in a box like this.

💡	**Tip** Tips and tricks appear like this.

Reader feedback

Feedback from our readers is always welcome. Let us know what you think about this book—what you liked or may have disliked. Reader feedback is important for us to develop titles that you really get the most out of.

To send us general feedback, simply send an e-mail to feedback@impacktpub.com, and mention the book title via the subject of your message.

If there is a topic that you have expertise in and you are interested in either writing or contributing to a book, see our author guide on www.impacktpub.com/authors.

Customer support

Now that you are the proud owner of an Impackt book, we have a number of things to help you to get the most from your purchase.

Errata

Although we have taken every care to ensure the accuracy of our content, mistakes do happen. If you find a mistake in one of our books—maybe a mistake in the text—we would be grateful if you would report this to us. By doing so, you can save other readers from frustration and help us improve subsequent versions of this book. If you find any errata, please report them by visiting http://www.impacktpub.com/support, selecting your book, clicking on the **errata submission form** link, and entering the details of your errata. Once your errata are verified, your submission will be accepted and the errata will be uploaded on our website, or added to any list of existing errata, under the Errata section of that title. Any existing errata can be viewed by selecting your title from http://www.impacktpub.com/support.

Piracy

Piracy of copyright material on the Internet is an ongoing problem across all media. At Impackt, we take the protection of our copyright and licenses very seriously. If you come across any illegal copies of our works, in any form, on the Internet, please provide us with the location address or website name immediately so that we can pursue a remedy.

Please contact us at copyright@impacktpub.com with a link to the suspected pirated material.

We appreciate your help in protecting our authors, and our ability to bring you valuable content.

Questions

You can contact us at questions@impacktpub.com if you are having a problem with any aspect of the book, and we will do our best to address it.

> 1
What is Time Management?

In this chapter, we will:

- > Define time management
- > Understand how different people think about time management
- > Identify some of the effects of poor time management
- > Enumerate the benefits of this concept called time management
- > Determine what people expect in a time management program

Time management is defined as the practice of controlling activities and events within available time. In order to do so, it is first necessary to understand and evaluate how time is currently being spent. The first exercise is to log activities, analyze how time is spent on various activities, determine your ideal allocation of time for each of these activity buckets, and plan and execute accordingly.

The limited view and the big picture

There is a story of five blind men who want to find out what an elephant is like. They come upon an elephant and reach out to touch it and satisfy their wants. Each one touches a different part of the elephant. One feels a leg and says, "An elephant is like a pillar." Another feels the side and says, "An elephant is like a wall." The third feels a tusk and says, "An elephant is like a spear." Another feels the tail and says, "An elephant is like a rope." The last feels an ear and says, "An elephant is like a fan." All of them are partially right but none are right. Likewise, people have different opinions as to what time management is. They all are partially right. They have a limited view. They don't have the big picture.

One way to determine what people think about time management is to ask a few general questions and collect answers. The questions can be:

- > What is the first thing that comes to your mind when you hear the phrase time management?
- > What does time management mean to you?
- > How will you benefit from better time management?

- What aspect of your time management skills do you most want to improve?
- How will your life change with better time management?

These are open-ended questions and form a good basis for a discussion.

The first benefit of opening the presentation with a question is that we are engaging the audience right from the start. Then again, there are no wrong answers with questions like these. When the participants see that all answers are accepted with no judgment, they are all the more willing to participate.

What *do* people think about the subject of time management? What *is* the first thing that comes to their minds when they come across the term time management? I have collected the following responses over the course of 8 years:

- Punctuality
- Meeting deadlines
- Being able to accomplish more
- Getting more done
- Completing all tasks on hand
- Self-discipline
- Using a planner/organizer well
- Well-ordered life
- Leisure
- Quality time
- Ability to do what I want
- Checking off items on a to-do list
- Peak performance
- Rating high on a performance review

This is not a complete list. There were some outliers and quite a few unprintable responses. This is a representative set of the responses that appeared most frequently.

Just as with the story about the five blind persons and the elephant, all of the previous statements are true but they're limited views and not the complete picture.

In most cases, the previous responses reflect what people are looking for in a time management system. They also represent the benefits people will reap when they improve their time management skills. In other words, people consider time management as a solution for a specific set of problems. Therefore, in order to define time management, the solution, we need to understand the problem or problems.

What are the problems? What are the symptoms that indicate the presence of the underlying problems?

Signs and results of poor time management

How can we recognize poor time management? It is easily recognized in others, for example, when tasks are not completed on time and when they arrive late to meetings and keep us waiting. It is easy to recognize in others the same negative traits that we may not recognize in ourselves!

Poor time management can be recognized in actions and in results. Sometimes, what is visible is merely the tip of the iceberg. In other cases, we may see neither the causes nor the results but there may be other signals to indicate poor time management. It is important to understand the actions, results, and signals that we watch for in others so that we may see them in our own behavior. Thus, when we recognize that we are behaving in a manner that indicates or leads to poor time management, we will be able to take steps to head off the negative results.

Is fever a symptom or the underlying problem? Is stress a symptom of the problem? Many of the issues a patient presents to a doctor are mere symptoms. Doctors do not merely treat symptoms. They probe to find and cure the underlying issues that present the symptoms. Likewise, many of the purported problems that we see in the time management arena are in fact symptoms.

Let's look at some of the signals that indicate poor time management, some of the underlying problems, and the results people with poor time management skills face.

What are the indicators of poor time management?

- Arriving late to meetings and appointments
- Missing appointments and meetings entirely
- Double-booked time slots, that is, conflicting schedules
- Often rescheduling appointments and meetings
- Not meeting deadlines
- Requesting deadline extensions
- Constantly switching between activities
- (Attempted) Multitasking
- Incomplete tasks
- Critical tasks not even started
- Forgotten tasks and chores
- Poor quality due to hurriedly slapped together things at the last minute
- Overflowing "In" tray
- E-mail inbox full of unread messages
- No spare time

What are the underlying problems?

- **Poor schedule management**: Proper use of a scheduling system with appointments, meetings, and scheduled events marked on the same calendar will ensure that there are no conflicting expectations on your time.
- **Poor task list (to-do list) management**: The fundamental purpose of time management is still to ensure that the current moment is being spent on the most appropriate activity. Making, pruning, and prioritizing a list of tasks is the best way to do so.
- **Poor planning**: The old adage is that if you fail to plan, you plan to fail.
- **Poor organization**: A place for everything and everything in its place, a time for every action and every action in its time.
- **Poor direction**: Many people operate without proper goals and objectives to give direction to their actions, that is, they drift without a sense of purpose.
- **Poor preparation**: Preparation ensures a smooth flow of actions.
- **Procrastination**: Procrastination is a terrible thief of productivity.
- **Not working fast enough**: This comes from inefficiency and the tendency to give in to distractions.
- **Poor time allocation**: Every task takes finite time. If you do not allocate enough time for any task, you will be scrambling to get things done at the last moment.
- **Poor management and control**: If the mandates from the management are contradictory and self-defeating, nothing can ever get done properly.
- **Not thinking things through**: When ramifications of decisions and actions are not considered sufficiently, they create new problems.
- **Poor self-discipline**: When everything else is in place, if tasks still do not get done in their time, the only one to blame is oneself. Dedication, diligence, and focus will help tasks get done.

What does poor time management lead to?

- Overwork
- Stress
- Sleep deprivation
- Tardiness
- Obesity
- Irritability
- Poor anger management
- A poor reputation, that is, people expect tardiness, schedule slippage, shoddy work, poor attitude, and so on

The problems may be stated in a different manner.

At work, corporations are trying to get more and more work done by fewer people and in less time. The easy target receiving all the blame for this phenomenon is "the economy", but this trend existed even during the great boom of the 90s. In good times as in bad times, many Machiavellian (that is, win at all costs) corporations do try to squeeze the most out of their employees. This may make economic sense in the short run, but in the long run, it burns employees out and makes them less productive.

On a personal level, people have too many things to do and not enough time to fit it all in. Modern conveniences and time-saving devices only seem to aggravate the situation. Just as a brand new kitchen cabinet gets filled in three days, time freed up by any new gadget is instantly snapped up by new chores and activities. The pressure just keeps mounting.

The outcome of all this pressure is that it has become the norm to work long hours. People are constantly chasing deadlines, are constantly under stress, and social life is painfully reduced.

Where does all the time go?

The result of this problem is not limited to reduced social life. Working insane hours leads to sleep deprivation, which in turn could lead to fatigue, irritability, and reduced life span.

When people are running from task to task, there is a tendency to merely play catch-up and be reactive. This leads to poor time management and disorganization. Poor time management and disorganization could compound the stressful frenzy already present: disorganization leads to loss of credibility, which in turn leads to loss of business or being passed over in promotion, and more stress. Stress could lead to ulcers, strokes, and heart attacks.

Benefits of time management

There are six areas of problems that good time management can solve:

- Schedule-related, that is, making and keeping appointments
- Productivity-related, that is, completing tasks as expected
- Competence-related, that is, professionalism in execution
- Quality-related, that is, attention to detail
- Health-related, that is, reduced stress and sufficient rest
- Life-related, that is, work/life balance

What does this mean? This means that people who manage their time well:

- Are punctual
- Meet deadlines
- Complete all tasks
- Give excellent quality
- Have their "In" trays and e-mail inboxes well in control

- Are organized
- Are prepared
- Are calm
- Are relaxed
- Have clear goals and work towards them
- Are healthy
- Are successful

Time management is a set of skills that instills priority, punctuality, performance, and productivity. Time management is a key element to success in life. This is the motivation to develop time management skills. Before learning any new skill, it is important to ask, "What's in it for me (WIIFM)?" This is the WIIFM factor for learning time management—it is a key element to success in life. In fact, Lee Iacocca, the automobile magnate, said, "The ability to concentrate and to use your time well is everything if you want to succeed in business—or almost anywhere else for that matter."

A definition of time management

What *is* time management? In order to answer this, let's move a step further. What is **time**? A physicist may respond that time is the fourth dimension and get technical about it, but that is not relevant in the context of time management.

Benjamin Franklin said, "Remember that time is money" in his article *Advice to a Young Tradesman*. He was right—up to a point. Think of time as money if it helps you understand its value. However, time is more than money. Money lost can be recovered, regained, earned again, begged, borrowed, or stolen. Time lost is gone forever.

Some people think twice about spending money on important things, and waste hours on trivial matters without a second thought. Isn't the time wasted worth as much as the money spent or saved?

What is the true value of time?

A person's earnings are measured in time. People get paid a certain amount every year, month, week, day, or hour. Is this what your time is worth?

Investments earn interest and dividends in time. Return on investment and interest paid on loans are measured in terms of "time value of money." Is this what your time is worth?

There is a natural tendency to value your time according to what you earn in that time. This is what your time is worth to someone else, the person who is paying your wages. What is your time worth to you?

Time is the essence of life. Every moment is priceless.

These, too, were Benjamin Franklin's words:

"Dost thou love life? Then do not squander time, for that is the stuff life is made of."

Charles Darwin said, "A man who dares waste one hour of time has not discovered the value of life."

> **Make a note**
> Time is the medium within which events and activities occur. Time management, therefore, is the control of events and activities in your life.

Obviously, not all events can be controlled. For example, you have no control over the weather, and, consequently, you have no control over activities that depend upon the weather. You do, however, have options. You have control over what you choose to do and how you choose to do it.

Let me expand this point a little more. If what you plan to do depends upon the weather, you must also make contingency plans. For example, if you wish to create a lawn party, you could create a backup plan to either set a rain date or be prepared to move the party indoors if the weather turns against you. Your choice puts some control within your hands.

Time management thus comes down to a choice. In fact, it is a continuous series of choices. The first choice is *what* events and activities you permit into your life. The second choice is *how* you tackle these events and activities.

Activity management

Let's explore further the previous definition of time management. At the highest level, there are three key words to inspect: **activities**, **events**, and **control**.

I use the term "activity" to denote something that requires action or something that is done. The subject is "active." Thus, activities include tasks, chores, duties, and routines. I use the term "event" to denote something that happens. The subject is a participant in or is affected by events. Thus, events include meetings, appointments, and group activities. For the purpose of this chapter, I will use the two terms interchangeably. The rest of this chapter is focused on the concept of controlling both activities and events, the concept of event control.

Event control

Peter Drucker, the noted management guru of the 20th century, famously said, "If you cannot measure it, you cannot manage it." We will be discussing time management metrics later in this book. For the present, let's look at identifying what we need to measure in order to control activities. The operating word here is "control." If you do not control the events in your life, the events in your life will control you.

The alternative to controlling events in your life is to be blown in any direction the winds of fate take you.

As mentioned before, you control the activities in your life by choice. The first choice is to decide *what* events and activities you permit into your life.

To what extent do you control the events you permit into your life? And how do you exercise the control? In other words, let's consider *what* events to control and *how* to control them.

There are several kinds of events:

> **Events that are totally out of your control**: These include the weather, the stock market, the economy, and so on. These also include situations that depend largely on the decisions and actions of those whom you cannot influence.

> **Complex events**: There are events wherein there are too many individual things that happen. You do not have the brainpower to consider them, let alone control them.

> **Events wherein your intervention would have negative consequences**: For example, just because you *can* control something does not mean that you *should* control it. For example, you need not exercise control over how your children behave every moment of the day. Only by letting children be children can you allow them to grow into wonderful beings.

Therefore, the first step is to identify different classes of events and decide how you will deal with them. In other words, if you can control certain events, decide whether it is worth doing so. If you cannot control certain events, decide whether it is worth the frustration of fretting about them or better to accept them and respond appropriately. For example, even if you cannot do anything about the weather, you can keep track of the forecasts and dress appropriately, carry an umbrella when needed, or lock down in anticipation of a severe storm.

How does one identify different classes of events? Every individual is subject to a different mix of events and event classes. The following section describes a process of identifying event classes and the time spent in each class of events.

Dividing the pies

There are 24 hours in a day. While what you do with these 24 hours on a particular day cannot be predicted to any accuracy, the average use of your time can be extrapolated from past experience.

In the world of finance, there is the concept of a budget. Every individual has a different apportioning of his or her salary depending on the gross amount, tax bracket, rent/mortgage, cost of living in a particular neighborhood, number of earners in the household, number of mouths to feed, and so on. Let's say that a representative gross salary allocation looks like this:

Activity	Allocation
Taxes	33.33%
Rent or mortgage	33.33%
Food	8.33%
Clothing	8.33%
Entertainment	8.33%
Discretionary cash	8.33%

This is extremely simplified in order to illustrate the concept. It does not, for instance, address savings or tithing. Nevertheless, the point is that an allocation or apportioning of income according to individual preferences exists. A further point is that unless you determine where your money is going, you will not have any control over your expenses. Therefore, the starting point is to keep track of your expense categories for a few months in order to understand your spending pattern. I call this post-ante division of the money pie.

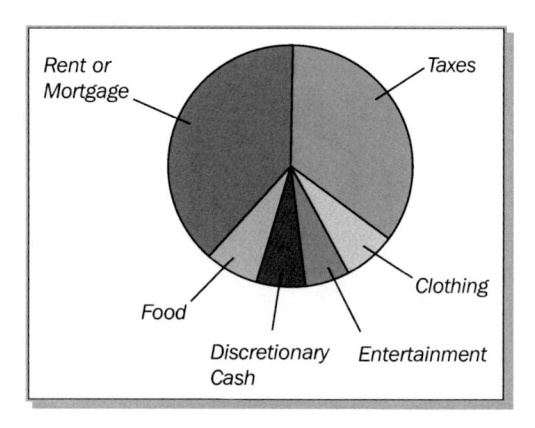

After you have captured this monthly information for a few months, you can then decide that you are spending too much in on category and not enough in another. You may not have too much control over what you spend in some categories such as taxes or rent or mortgage unless you take significant steps such as tax strategies or downsizing your residence. You will much more control over categories such as entertainment, savings, and discretionary expenses. You can then create a new allocation/apportioning table that you feel is more suitable for your temperament. I call this ex-ante division of the money pie.

The term ex-ante refers to doing something in advance, and post-ante refers to doing something afterwards.

Let's apply the same concept to time. It is useful to know where your time went (that is, ex-post) in order to estimate where your time will go (that is, ex-ante). A representative post-ante division of time may look like this:

Activity	Allocation
Sleep	33%
Work	33%
Personal grooming	8.33%
Commute	8.33%
Chores	8.33%
Discretionary time	8.33%

Again, as with the money example, you can capture this information over several days and analyze the data to determine how you will change the allocation. For example, you may decide to reduce your sleep time and spend some time in working out. You may decide to be efficient in personal grooming and reduce the corresponding allocation. You may find a new route or public transportation option in order to reduce the commute time. As you can understand, you can manipulate this allocation table in a multitude of ways after you know where your time is going. The first step is to understand where your time is going right now.

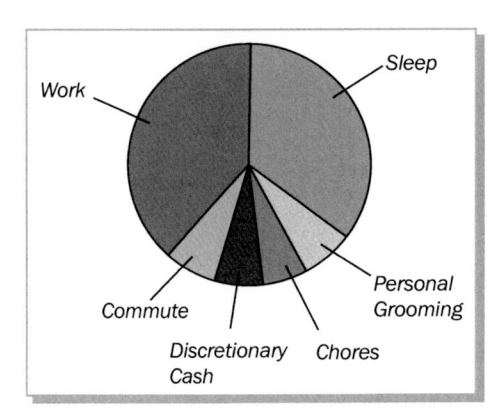

Exercise

Your first assignment, should you choose to accept it, is to keep an honest time log for 10 days. Keep track of everything you do. Classify each activity so as to only track aggregates, that is, roll up the time spent to the categories. Therefore, you will not need to know that you spent 25 minutes on a train and 30 minutes in a bus if you know that you spent 55 minutes commuting.

Actually, to make things more interesting, predict what you expect the results to be. Create a table or pie chart with categories and estimated time usage in each category. Do this before the first day's activity log.

This exercise is one of the most difficult things to do because it requires you to be totally honest with yourself. Please do not sweep dust under a rug and pretend that all is well. If necessary, take steps to ensure that no one else can see your log if doing so gives you a certain level of comfort.

Brutal honesty is the only way to know yourself best.

The second part of the exercise is to analyze the time log. After you have kept a time log for about 10 days, create a representative table with the 10-day average for each category. Compare this with the prediction you made before you began to log your activities. What are the differences? What are the surprises? Are you pleasantly surprised or horrified?

You will be astonished by some of the ineffective things you do right now. I certainly was when I first went through this exercise!

I still go through this exercise periodically to make sure that I am not slipping into old bad habits. I also take the opportunity to review changes in my routine due to changing demands on my time. For example, when my older son obtained his driving license and I got him a car, I did not need to shuttle him between his activities anymore. This freed up some of my time and allowed me to take on more activities.

The third part of the exercise is to create a new time budget. Now that you know where your time is being spent, bring some of the areas under control. Eliminate some of the categories and reduce the time allotted to some of the others. Peter Drucker said, "There is nothing so useless as doing efficiently that which should not be done at all." You can also increase the time allocation for the better categories. For example, spend more time on improving yourself.

Finally, after you have created the new time allocation chart, follow this chart rigorously for at least 21 days. There is scientific evidence to show that the human body takes at least 21 days to adapt to a new routine and make it the norm. Therefore, force the new routine until it becomes the habit. Then you will not have to consciously work on it anymore.

Discussion and illustration

If you are conducting the preceding exercise in a training session, to encourage participation, ask the trainees to present their views on time management, list the problems that they face due to poor time management, and list the benefits of good time management. Throw out definitions of time and time management and invite their comments. Take a contrarian position, that is, benefits of poor time management, and have them argue with you. Keep track of the responses and comments. The same discussion may be repeated at the end of the workshop to see whether there is any change in position as a result of the workshop.

Illustrate the concepts with stories of successful people. Show how proper time management was the key element that vaulted their heroes to the top of their careers. Take examples from different industries and cultures.

Summary

Time management is a solution to a set of problems related to priority, punctuality, performance, and productivity.

Poor time management leads to dealing poorly with scheduled events such as meetings, appointments and deadlines, build-up of incomplete tasks, poor reputation, over work, sleep deprivation, stress, poor relationships, and poor health. Poor time management sets one up for failure.

Effective time management results in a well-organized life, time for personal activities, relaxation, and quality time with friends and family, good, and excellent health. Effective time management sets one up for success.

Time is the medium within which events occur. Time management is, therefore, control over events and activities in your life.

Event control includes identifying, classifying, and budgeting time for activities. This begins with an event log to determine the demands made on your time.

Keep a time log to note where your time is being spent. Use the time log to identify inefficiencies and ineffective use of time. Reallocate your time to reduce wastage. Follow the new schedule diligently for at least three weeks before it becomes the new habit, the new norm, and the new pattern of behavior and time usage.

> 2
Setting Goals

In this chapter, we will work on the foundations of good time management. We understand from the previous chapter that time management is the result of controlling the activities in our lives. We must now determine what activities we control and how we should go about doing so. This chapter shows that the first question should not be "what" or "how", but "why." When we know why we should do something, there is less resistance and more enthusiasm. We can also filter out activities that take our time but do not add value to our lives. The primary filters are our values and goals. We will explore the process of developing and stating goals. In order to have a consistent set of goals, they must have a strong foundation in values and beliefs. Therefore, we will build a value system to anchor and align our goals and daily activities. In this chapter, we will see how value systems determine goals and how aligning daily tasks to goals and intermediate steps ensure congruence in our lives.

Values

There is a story about an army corps of engineers who went to clear a forest. As trained and disciplined as they were, they went about in an organized and efficient manner and cleared the area in a very short time. Naturally, they were quite proud of it, until they got word from the commanders—they had cleared the wrong forest!

Therefore, before we get all fired up and dig deep into the mechanics of time management, let's make sure that we are clearing the right forest.

Underlying every action is a purpose. Purpose drives time management decisions such as prioritization and delegation. It answers the "why" questions such as "Why is this task important?" or "Why should this task be done before that task?" Purpose should form the basis for goal setting.

Underlying purpose is value. Value, the moral compass and spark of integrity that illuminates every soul, ensures that your goals do not conflict with conscience and pragmatism.

In his book *The 10 Natural Laws of Successful Time and Life Management*, Hyrum Smith introduced his concept of the productivity pyramid or personal fulfilment pyramid. In this, Smith explained that every action we take must relate to our goals or the intermediary steps that we would take to reach our goals, and our goals must align with our values.

The word "value" refers to the perceived worth of something. When we talk about moral values, we are ascribing monetary worth to non-monetary and intangible concepts.

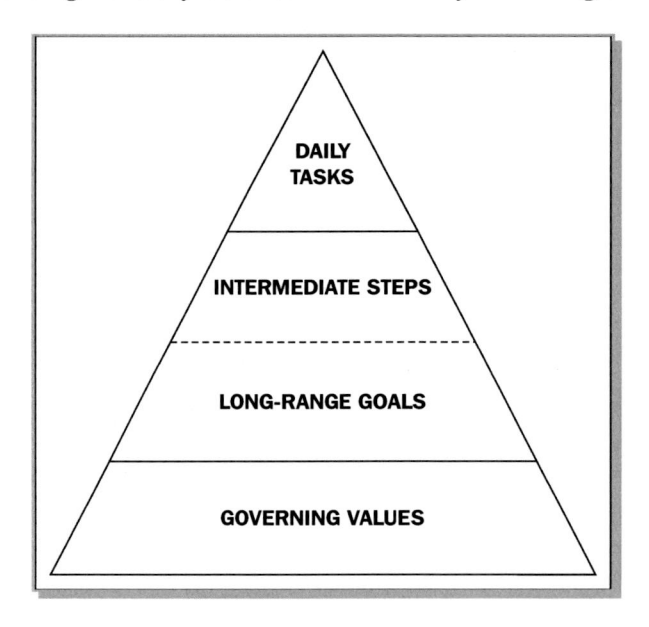

```
        DAILY
        TASKS

    INTERMEDIATE STEPS

    LONG-RANGE GOALS

    GOVERNING VALUES
```

Time management involves controlling the events in our lives. The two aspects of event control are deciding *what* to do and *how* to do it. Yet, before we can decide *what* to do, we must have a basis for the decision, otherwise the decision is arbitrary and subjective, that is, if we had to make the same kind of decision again, we may not decide in the same manner. There would be no consistency in our behavior, which is not a good indicator of reliability or professionalism.

Value system

What would be a good basis for decision making? How do we ensure that our decisions are consistent? The foundation of any kind of decision-making process is a *value system*. This is the set of beliefs and virtues that direct our behavior. Our goals and actions must align with this value system, otherwise, we will constantly face conflicts.

For example, we may have a goal to be successful and be the recognized expert in a particular field of work. At what price will we accept our achievement? In Niccolo Machiavelli's *The Prince*, he encourages one to "win at all costs." Would we? Would our conscience accept such a victory, or would winning at all costs lead to an empty victory and a bad taste in the mouth? Where should we draw the line?

Thus, our goals are constrained by our values.

Values include traits such as:

> - Honesty
> - Humility

- Generosity
- Respect
- Politeness
- Fairness
- Gentleness
- Non-violence
- Justice
- Sportsmanship
- Chivalry
- Professionalism
- Diligence
- Persistence
- Hard work
- Perseverance
- Single-mindedness of purpose
- Focus
- Excellence
- Quality
- Courage

A value system is a *set of consistent values*. The operative word here is "consistent." A set of values is consistent if the individual values in the set do not contradict each other. For example, the values of absolute honesty and diplomacy (with its penchant for white lies) do not resound with each other. Non-violence and fighting for what we believe in cannot coexist.

Another point of consistency is that values must be followed without exception in all situations. If values are followed only when convenient or advantageous and not followed otherwise, there is no consistency.

How do we go about building a value set?

We really do not *create* a value set as much as we *assemble* one from the beliefs and virtues that have been instilled in us from early life. These are sometimes destroyed when role-models behave contrary to the values they project, often with a "Do as I say, not as I do" attitude. Nevertheless, as rational and discerning human beings, we can identify the values that we should follow in order to have a well-balanced and satisfactory life.

Benefit

What is the value of a value system? What is in this for you?

A value system is the first filter of activities. As time is a very precious commodity, you need an objective basis to ensure that your time is not being wasted. If you ensure that everything that you include in your life, every activity that you make time for, agrees with your value system, at the least you will have the satisfaction that your time is not wasted. Only activities that align with your value system will be included in your life.

For example, the following is Benjamin Franklin's *List of Defined Virtues*. This is included here as an illustration:

1. **Temperance** – *eat not to dullness; drink not to elation.*

2. **Silence** – *Speak not but what may benefit others or yourself; avoid trifling conversation.*

3. **Order** – *Let all your things have their places; let each part of your business have its time.*

4. **Resolution** – *Resolve to perform what you ought; perform without fail what you resolve.*

5. **Frugality** – *Make no expense but to do good to others or yourself; that is, waste nothing.*

6. **Industry** – *Lose no time; be always employed in something useful; cut off all unnecessary actions.*

7. **Sincerity** – *Use no hurtful deceit; think innocently and justly; speak accordingly.*

8. **Justice** – *Wrong none by doing injuries; or omitting the benefits of your duty.*

9. **Moderation** – *Avoid extremes; forbear resenting injuries so much as you think they deserve.*

10. **Cleanliness** – *Tolerate no uncleanliness in body, clothes, or habitation.*

11. **Tranquility** – *Be not disturbed at trifles or at accidents common or unavoidable.*

12. **Chastity** – *Rarely use venery but for health or offspring, never to dullness, weakness, or the injury of your own or another's peace or reputation.*

Exercise

The first exercise in this section of this chapter is a discussion. Ask your employees what they understand about values, value systems, and virtues. Use general questions to obtain the most diverse and thoughtful responses. One way to guide this discussion is to present the list of values stated previously and invite comments and additions to the list.

The second exercise in this chapter is to create a plausible value system that your employees can follow and use to anchor and align their goals and daily tasks. They may use the following steps to create the value system:

1. Create a list of traits and virtues. Make the list as large as possible.
2. For each item, give a short sentence to show how you relate to the item. For example, in Benjamin Franklin's value system, he relates the value "Order" to "Let all your things have their places; let each part of your business have its time."
3. From this list, pick traits and virtues that resound with your nature. Pick items that you value and respect.
4. Check the list for consistency. If any of the items contradict each other, pick the one that would be consistent with most of the other items in the list.
5. Rewrite the final list with the associated descriptions as your value set.

A shortcut to this process may be to take an existing value system, for example, Ben Franklin's *List of Virtues*, and edit it as appropriate.

Goals

Research tells us that fewer than 3 percent of Americans have written goals, and less than 1 percent periodically review and restate their goals in response to changing conditions in their lives. What this means is that most people do not have clear directions or destinations in their lives. They go where the winds blow them with no say in the matter. They have no control over their destiny. Swami Vivekananda, the Indian mystic and philosopher, stated, "Take the whole responsibility on your own shoulders and know that you are the creator of your own destiny."

About 10 years ago, there was an article in the *Fast Company* magazine about the "1953 Yale Study of Goals." This study found that people who write down specific goals for their future are far more likely to be successful than those who have either unwritten goals or no specific goals at all.

Mark McCormack, author of *What They Don't Teach You at Harvard Business School*, wrote, "All successful people have goals, and outstanding high achievers have clearly defined written goals."

Taking control over our destiny begins with having clear goals and objectives.

Why don't most people state their goals?

According to Brian Tracy (*Success Through Goal-Setting*), there are five reasons why people don't set goals:

1. **They are simply not serious**: People do not achieve anything remarkable unless they get "serious" about it.

2. **They don't understand the importance of goals**: People who come from successful families understand the value of goals early in life. Others grow up with the idea that goals are not even part of a normal existence.

3. **They don't know how to do it**: Goal setting is not included in standard education syllabus.

4. **Fear of rejection**: The moment that people declare a worthwhile goal, someone steps up and tells them that they cannot achieve it and why. This destructive criticism causes the fear of rejection.

5. **Fear of failure**: People do not set goals because they are afraid they may fail. Fear of failure is the single greatest obstacle to success.

There are other reasons, too. The following reasons are related to experience, or lack thereof, and therefore, your employees will greatly benefit from knowing them so as to recognize them for what they are and be able to recover from these negative behavior patterns:

1. **Too busy to set goals**: People are constantly fighting fires and moving from crisis to crisis. Since they do not have goals and plans, everything that they do is unplanned and, quite often, unexpected.

2. **Inability to decide**: Some people want so many things that they do not know which of them to pick as a single goal or the first goal to pursue. This also leads to uncertainty. They are unsure of what they have decided upon and constantly change their minds. This is what I call the restaurant syndrome. Many people at restaurants look at what people around them are having and wish they had ordered for the same. This prevents them from enjoying what they had on their plates! Likewise, after declaring a goal, they look at the goals of people around them and change their minds.

3. **Fear of success**: People are afraid that if they succeed, they will have to leave behind their existing friends and circles in order to hobnob with people at a new level. There is also the "Winner's Curse", that is, success leading to raised expectations of performance by peers and bosses and therefore having to work harder.

4. **Uncomfortable with change**: Even with all its negative qualities, people are comfortable with the status quo. They fear the unknown and are unwilling to do anything that will expose them to their fears.

Your employees must set goals in order to function effectively, efficiently, and consistently. It is important to address the reasons why people do not set, state, clarify, or write their goals in order to get your employees to identify their unique situation(s) and take action. As most psychiatrists will agree, most people are in denial when it comes to their problems even though they readily accept other people's problems. When your employees recognize their reasons for not setting goals, they will have taken the first step to solving them.

The barriers and objections must be examined and appropriately countered. In order to change a person's mindset, behavior, and habit, it is more important to convince, persuade, and influence than it is to state, prove, or force. William Shakespeare said, "Your gentleness shall force more than your force move us to gentleness" (*As You Like It*, Act II, Scene 7).

The best way to set goals is to see what we value most. We can pursue several goals in different areas at the same time. For example, we can simultaneously have personal goals and professional goals. We may also have several personal goals in various categories, such as:

- Health (lose weight, run a marathon)
- Family and friends (strengthen relationship, get married)
- Hobbies (build a model, write a book)
- Travel (take a cruise, visit exotic places)

At the same time, we may have several professional goals in various categories, such as:

- Performance (improve sales pitch, be prompt on follow up)
- Career development (take a training course, get certification in a relevant skill)
- Self-promotion (write white papers, set standards)

On the other hand, having multiple goals within the same category dilutes our focus. We can, however, have a series of goals that we achieve one at a time.

Benefit

What is the value of stating our goals? People relate very well to benefits because they constantly ask, "What's In It For Me?" This is referred to as the *WIIFM* question.

Here are some of the benefits of having one or more goals in place:

- **Motivation**: A clear goal will inspire you to take action to achieve it.
- **Destination**: You will have the end in mind and know precisely what you are striving for.
- **Direction**: The goal ensures that all the steps you take will lead in the same direction to the same end.
- **Purpose**: A sense of purpose leads to achievement.
- **Justification**: You can justify decisions and actions in the context of the goal.

SMART goals

Let's look at the value of clearly formulated goals. Take a look at the following two examples:

1. Goal: To lose weight.
2. Goal: To reduce my weight by 15 pounds in 6 weeks.

The first goal is very nebulous. It is a general goal.

The second is a SMART goal. SMART goals are:

- **Specific**: The goal is detailed, unambiguous, and addresses any questions that may arise. When a goal is specific, there is a greater chance of accomplishing it when compared to a general, nebulous goal. A specific goal is created as the answer to questions such as:
    - What must be accomplished?
    - When must it be done by?
    - Who is involved in the accomplishment?
    - Where should the work be done?
    - How is the work to be done (details, steps)?
    - Why is this important (WIIFM)?
- **Measurable**: The goal is stated such that there exists an exact method of measuring progress towards the attainment of the goal.
- **Attainable**: It is *possible* to attain the goal as stated. In other words, it is not outside the realm of possibility. For an extremely overweight person to state a goal of beating the current world record in running a mile is ludicrous. However, for the second-best mile runner in the world to make such a goal puts it in the realm of possibility.
- **Realistic**: Even if a goal were possible, that is, attainable, for it to be attained, one must be both *willing* and *able* to work at it. A realistic goal is one that is not only *possible* but also *probable* or *likely*.
- **Timely**: The goal must have a finite time within which it is to be achieved. If there is no time limit, there is no sense of urgency.

Benefits of having SMART goals

What is the value of having SMART goals? What are the benefits (that is, WIIFM)?

There is a degree of confidence that we will achieve SMART goals as opposed to a nebulous goal. By ensuring that the goal is both possible, that is, it is in the realm of possibility, and probable, that is, we are willing and able to work at it, we have put it within our reach. With the proper time limit, we have placed bounds within which it must be achieved. Many things do not happen unless there is proper time restriction. With proper motivation, it is very likely that we will achieve a SMART goal.

Employees will reap the greatest benefits from setting and achieving SMART goals during their performance reviews. SMART goals become the yardsticks against which managers can measure performance and progress of their employees. When the goals are timed to be achieved within the review periods, when the goals are specific and realistic, when their progress can be measured, they can be achieved. This will make it easier for managers to evaluate their employees periodically.

Exercise

The first part of this exercise is a discussion of the benefits of setting goals. The previous list, motivation, destination, direction, purpose, and justification, is not exhaustive. Can your employees come up with more benefits? Understanding benefits, the WIIFM factor, encourages your employees to question whether it is worth their time to do something. One of the points introduced in the next chapter is the *Pareto Principle*, the famous *80-20 rule*, which says that 80 percent of the value is gleaned from 20 percent of the actions. When your employees understand the value of an action, they will tend to favor actions that give more value.

Let me set the context of this exercise with a story:

> *Many years ago, a wanderer came upon two workers who were digging a large hole in the ground. The two were asked what they were doing as they started digging a ditch. One man says, "Digging a ditch." The second man says, "I'm building a cathedral."*

When we see the value of what we are doing and how it will relate to the larger picture, our attitude towards the task changes. Thus, it is very important to make sure your employees know that their every action contributes to the success of the entire group and organization.

The second exercise in this section of the chapter is to have your employees create one or more SMART goals in one or more categories in both personal and professional arenas:

1. The first step in this exercise is to create a potential set of nebulous goals.
2. The second step is to associate the potential goals with values from the value system (created in the first exercise in this chapter).
3. The third step is to eliminate potential goals that are not anchored to specific values.
4. Of the remaining potential goals, classify them according to personal and professional goals, and also place them into categories such as health, hobby, or family bonding.
5. If any category has more than one goal, pick one (for now).
6. Convert every potential goal remaining in the list into a SMART goal by making it Specific, Measurable, Attainable, Relevant, and Timely.

Finally, just as it is important to determine that the value system is internally consistent, that is, none of the values contradict each other, it is equally important to determine that the goals do not lead one in opposing directions. Ask your employees to check their goal sets for internal consistency.

Action plans

Peter Drucker, the great management guru of the 20th century, declared, "If you fail to plan, you plan to fail." While the mere fact that we have created a plan does not automatically guarantee success, the absence of a plan makes success even more unlikely.

Imagine this: you decide to build an extension to your house. You rush to the lumberyard and hardware store, get a load of beams, sheets, and nails, and start assembling them together. Plans? Blueprints? Who needs them, right? Or would you begin with a plan, create a blueprint, get the necessary permits and approvals, determine the sequence of actions, procure the hardware needed for each stage, and proceed in a logical manner? The results will speak for the efficacy of either method.

Visions, goals, and objectives are intangible. Only results are tangible. Therefore, when we look retrospectively at something we have achieved, visions, goals, and objectives do not matter: only results matter.

How do we convert visions, goals, and objectives into results? How do we achieve what we set out to?

Actions create results, although not all the results may be to our satisfaction. *Right actions* create the desired results. Right actions achieve goals and objects. An **action plan** is a sequence of actions that lead to the goal.

Short-term objectives

A **goal** is often referred to as an end or a destination. Using a destination as a metaphor for a goal, let's look at finding a path from our current location to the destination. Many vehicles today come with a **Global Positioning Satellite (GPS)** based navigation system. Even if your particular vehicle does not have one, many after-market and hand-held devices, including smart phones, give you the ability to find a path from the current location to a destination expressed as an address or positional coordinates. There are also many web-based solutions such as www.mapquest.com, www.maps.google.com, and www.maps.yahoo.com. For the moment, let's ignore those solutions and consider how we would find a route from where you are to a place you would like to get to.

Let's consider three approaches that we may take:

> **Forward tracking**: Set out in the direction of the destination. In most cases, we will not be able to go in the exact direction. We will have to go in an approximate direction and make course corrections as we go along. To make matters easy, we identify places where we would make the course changes ahead of time.

> **Backtracking**: Work back from the destination and identify intermediate destinations we would touch on our way. As we move forwards, we use these intermediate destinations as milestones to ensure that we are on the right path.

> **Known-road strategy**: Suppose there is one road that we know is nearby and leads almost until the destination. In this case, all we need to know is the steps to get to the known road from where we are and the steps from where we need to leave the known road until the destination.

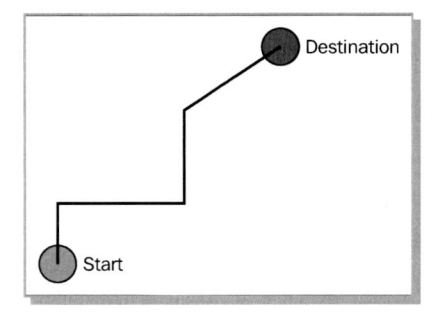

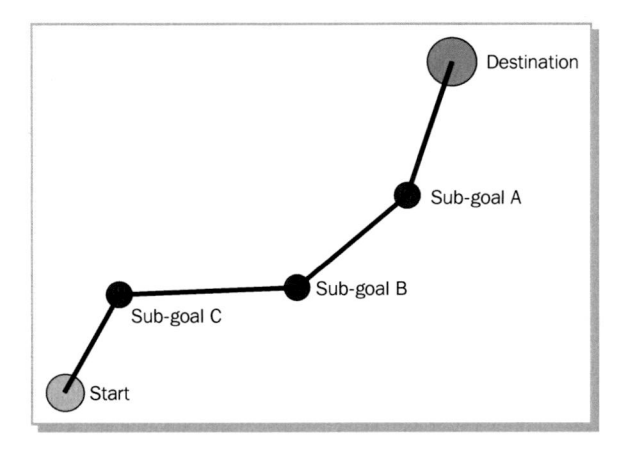

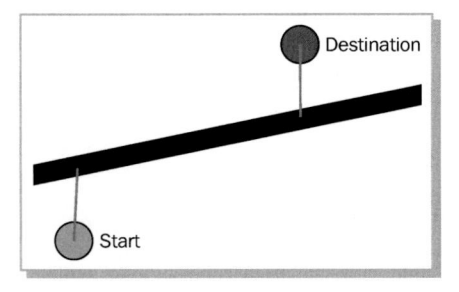

Of these three approaches, the one most commonly used is the middle one, backtracking. However, the most efficient strategy is the last one, the known-road strategy. In the last method, we are extending a known solution and therefore reducing risk.

When we break down a goal into constituent intermediary sub-goals, we must try to use as many known pieces as we can. This will reduce the stress in the implementation and make for a smooth path.

What is the value of an action plan? What is the WIIFM factor?

An action plan removes doubts and similar obstacles that would otherwise prevent you from reaching goals. When we know the sequence of steps and actions that will lead to the goal, many of the risks and uncertainties are eliminated.

Daily activities

There are three kinds of activities in every individual's day:

- Routine or mundane activities
- Planned activities
- Unplanned activities

Of these, the routine or mundane activities happen as a matter of course. These activities require no thought either for inclusion in the daily list of tasks or for execution. The exceptions to these are things that we are trying to change, either in creating new habits or in trying to eliminate some old ones.

The unplanned activities come from external sources. These are interruptions and disruptions. For example, your friend may call you and ask for your help in dealing with a personal emergency. Your car may breakdown and may require immediate attention. The manner in which we respond to unplanned demands on our time depends both on the nature of the interruption and the value of the current task.

The middle set of activities, the planned activities, should be the day-to-day implementation of an action plan in order to take us closer to our intermediate steps towards an ultimate goal.

What is the value of aligning daily tasks with goals and values? What is the WIIFM factor?

The Merriam-Webster dictionary defines *congruence* as "the quality or state of agreeing, coinciding, or being congruent." *Congruent* is further defined as "superposable so as to be coincident throughout." The operating concept is *being* coincident.

When creating goals and action plans, it is important to be congruent.

What does it mean to be congruent? It means that our daily tasks, our goals and the intermediary steps, and our core values are all coincident and consistent. Since our goals stem from our values, our daily activities, our intermediary steps, our goals, and our values are in alignment. As Hyrum Smith said, "When your daily activities reflect your governing values, you experience inner peace" (Law #3, *The 10 Natural Laws for Successful Time and Life Management, Hyrum Smith*).

Exercise

The first part of this exercise is a discussion. Ask your employees what they see as the biggest benefit (WIIFM) of an action plan and the value of aligning daily tasks with goals and values.

The second part of this exercise is an extension of the previous one.

Ask your employees to take one of the goals they have created from the previous exercise and create action plans using the three methods, forward tracking, backtracking, and known-road strategy. Ask them to evaluate the action plans for ease of implementation.

They must ultimately have action plans for all the goals that they created in the previous exercise.

Summary

As time management has been defined as activity management, that is, your time is managed when you have control over the activities and events in your life, the first step towards successful time management is to control the mix of events in your life. What this means is that you must evaluate each activity that comes your way and decide whether or not you allow it to occupy your time. In order to be objective and consistent in filtering activities, you must have a basis for your decision.

If you have a set of clearly stated goals for each facet of your life, you have the ability to test every activity that comes your way and see whether it leads you towards or away from the appropriate goal. Reject the activities that will not help you accomplish your goals.

A value system is a set of beliefs, behavior traits, and virtues that govern your thoughts, decisions, and actions. Create an internally consistent set of values and live by them.

When you create a set of goals, anchor each goal to one or more values. For each goal, identify the steps that you must take in order to reach it.

Your daily planned activities must lead you towards the intermediate steps of appropriate goals. When your daily activities align with your goals and values, you will achieve inner peace.

Some people believe that when life is planned down to excruciating details, such a life lacks spontaneity and excitement. This is a very important point of discussion in this chapter.

Is planning detrimental? When is planning detrimental? What level of planning is acceptable? What level of planning is required?

The old adage is, "If you fail to plan, you plan to fail." Success comes from good planning and good execution.

Underlying plans are goals and objectives. Underlying goals are the core values. Some people consider core values as very personal and private matters. This could be a touchy discussion. However, time management is a life skill. It is an essential part of personal development and self-discipline. To ensure that the lessons are well learned, it is important to explore touchy matters and sacrifice some sacred cows. Therefore, take a controversial stand, invite comments, and encourage an active discussion.

The value of this chapter is this: all successful people have goals, and outstanding high achievers have clearly defined written goals. Without the encouragement or even awareness about the benefits of clearly written goals, a very small part of the population (about 3 percent) formulates and states goals. Mark McCormack found that people who have clear, stated goals earn up to 10 times as much as those who do not. By stating and reiterating the value of goals, it is hoped that employees take on a habit that helps them succeed. In addition, Hyrum Smith believed that goals that are anchored in core values have a greater chance of being achieved. Finally, aligning daily activities to goals, which are, in turn, aligned to core values, leads to inner peace.

History has many examples of successful people who had clearly stated goals. Benjamin Franklin, Sir Winston Churchill, President Dwight D. Eisenhower, and Earl Nightingale are excellent subjects of discussion.

The next chapter introduces the first of the two critical processes in time management, managing the to-do list. While we would like to focus on the tasks that will lead to our ultimate goals, there are many things that come our way. Managing the to-do list is crucial to our ability to achieve goals in life.

3

Task Management

In this chapter, we will address the primary question relating to time management: *What is the best use of my time right now?* In the previous chapter, we saw that the "why" question (expressed as values and goals) could be used to filter out unwanted tasks. We shall now see how to address the "what" question.

Time is a limited resource. Indeed, at the most limiting level of detail, the only time available to us is now, the current instant in time. There is only one such instant, and it is but a fleeting instant. This is why it is important to decide what is important enough to occupy the instant over everything else that vies for our attention. In the previous chapter, we showed you how to relate daily tasks to intermediary steps towards achieving long-range goals that are in agreement with our value system. However, they are not the only kind of tasks that occupy our time. There are routine tasks such as those we undertake to maintain our physical health, hygiene, and well-being.

There are required tasks that come with the roles we have both in our personal and professional capacities. For example, in our role as parents, we may have to transport our offspring between tasks. In our role as volunteers at churches, religious organizations, social organizations, we may be required to call on many people to raise funds or to increase participation. In our professional roles, we may have to take care of a large amount of paperwork, which does not directly contribute to our area of work but keeps the company alive. There are obligatory tasks, things that we are obliged to do as a result of our position in society and the relationships we have with others. There are optional tasks that we could choose to undertake under certain conditions or in available time. There are tasks that we desire to take on. All these tasks have a legitimate demand upon our time. **Task management** is a process that allows us to objectively and consistently select the activity that gives us the most value for the moment. Activity management allows us to answer the most important question in time management: *what is the best use of my time right now?*

There are four steps in this process:

1. List tasks.
2. Prioritize the list.
3. Filter the tasks on the list.
4. Pick the highest priority activity that survives the filtration.

A beginner will try to combine some of the steps. For example, it is very tempting to attempt to prioritize and filter tasks even while adding them to the list. It does not work. The process is very objective when the steps are separate. Combining steps makes the process subjective and inconsistent.

The process of activity management can be seen in the following flow chart:

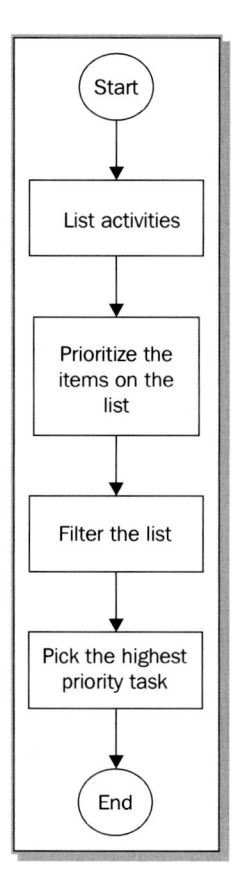

```
        Start
          │
          ▼
   ┌──────────────┐
   │List activities│
   └──────────────┘
          │
          ▼
   ┌──────────────┐
   │ Prioritize the│
   │ items on the │
   │     list     │
   └──────────────┘
          │
          ▼
   ┌──────────────┐
   │Filter the list│
   └──────────────┘
          │
          ▼
   ┌──────────────┐
   │Pick the highest│
   │ priority task │
   └──────────────┘
          │
          ▼
         End
```

These steps will be explained in the following sections.

Activity lists

It may be obvious, but so many people forget how valuable lists can be as a time management aid. Taking a small amount of time to develop an activity list or a simple plan for a day, week, or month can save you time in the long run. Indeed, developing this list is the first step in planning, and self-help guru Brian Tracy said, "Every minute you spend in planning saves 10 minutes in execution; this gives you a 1000 percent Return on Energy!"

The to-do list

Many years ago, I worked with a very methodical person. He was very detail-oriented and meticulously crossed off items on a checklist as he completed them. I argued with him about the value of memory over physical lists. He had a very simple answer: *paper remembers what the mind could forget*. Today, many years after this incident, I see the wisdom of his answer. We have limited capabilities for keeping track of many things simultaneously. We are subject to distractions. Memory is not infallible.

An activity list is either a physical (that is, paper) or an electronic (that is, computer, smart phone, tablet, or web-based) list that keeps track of things that must be done.

The first question many students ask at this time is: what does this list track? What kinds of items would we track on such a list?

It is not necessary to track *routine* tasks, that is, things that would get done without even having to think about them. Everything else—absolutely everything else—goes on the list. This includes *required* tasks, *optional* tasks, *obligatory* tasks, *desired* tasks, and *goal-directed* tasks. Indeed, paper remembers what the mind could forget.

As mentioned earlier, it is important to add items to the list without judgment or attempt to prioritize and filter the activity. Prioritization and filtration are subsequent steps in the process of activity management.

The next question many students ask is about the number of lists: is one list enough or do we track different kinds of tasks in different lists?

There are several schools of thought on this issue. I generally present some of them in my workshops and have the students discuss the merits and demerits thereof. It is not merely a matter of opinion: different situations, work cultures, or personalities work best with specific activity list strategies, therefore it is best to know them all and use the one that is best suitable for the situation, workplace, or personality. In my own case, I switch between two different strategies depending on my current focus.

The early time management systems, for example Benjamin Franklin's, used a single list. Alan Lakein, a pioneer in modern time management concepts, used a single list but added a notation to distinguish between required tasks (A), optional tasks (B), and wish list (C). David Allen (*Getting Things Done*) recommends different "buckets" each to hold a different class of tasks depending on role and objective.

I have two recommendations. The first strategy uses two lists, one for professional or work-related tasks and the other for everything else. The second also uses two lists, one for tasks or activities that are related to long-range goals and the other for everything else. I pick the strategy that best suits my situation at work. If my profession demands more of my attention, for example, at the end of a fiscal quarter or when I am trying to meet quotas, I use the first strategy. At all other times, I use the second strategy.

Exercises

There are three exercises in this section of this chapter.

The first exercise is a discussion to identify the merits and demerits of a single activity list versus the use of multiple activity lists according to role and objective. This can be an open-ended discussion allowing the creation of new strategies or modifying existing ones. The objective of this exercise is to find each student one or two strategies that they may use.

I believe that no single time management system works for everyone all the time. The objective of this first exercise is to enable students to begin formulating a system that would work for their specific situation such that they have a greater inclination to stick to it. Indeed, when they create a system that fits them like a well-tailored suit, they have a sense of ownership and an incentive to make it work.

The second exercise in this chapter is to make a list of things to do. For the purpose of this exercise, have your students focus on a single list. However, in order to build this list, it is necessary to think about required tasks, obligatory tasks, optional tasks, roles, objectives, needs, wants, wishes, desires, and so on. These thoughts will trigger associations and the list will grow rapidly. At this point in time, the exercises already completed in terms of goals and action plans will also contribute to the list of tasks to be accomplished.

The third exercise is to analyze the lists created in the second exercise and discuss whether it is better to have a single list or divide the list into two or more lists. There is no right answer, and the students will benefit from contrasting points of view.

Prioritization

Pixar's animated movie *The Incredibles* has a very interesting message to convey. In one scene, Helen Parr tells her son Dash, "Everyone's special, Dash," to which her son responds, "Which is another way of saying no one is." In another scene, the super villain Syndrome reveals that he is going to sell his inventions to everyone, so that everyone can have superpowers. He then says, "When everyone's super, no one is!" Contrast this with George Orwell's slogan from "Animal Farm," "All animals are equal; some are more equal than others."

If every task on a to-do list were of equal importance, it is impossible to decide which of them should be done next. Any arbitrary criterion used to decide and pick a task would be just that—arbitrary. All tasks cannot be special or equal. Some are, indeed, more equal than others. The priority of each task must be set apart from other so as to have a clear way of selecting one of them.

Many managers also fall into the trap of becoming one-trick ponies, the only trick they know being pressure tactics. They apply pressure on their employees by deeming every task to be of highest priority and demanding immediate response on everything they ask for. The effect of this pressure tactic is that there is no clear priority on individual tasks. The employees get stressed out and quality suffers yielding poor results for the effort expended.

There are several strategies for prioritizing tasks. Before I enumerate these strategies, describe how they work, and show their similarities and differences, I will introduce a very useful evaluation technique. Priority, urgency, and importance are subjective attributes. They depend on individual values and ideals. Different people would prioritize the same list of tasks in different orders. However, it is important that individuals should be consistent in the way that they evaluate tasks such that the same list of tasks on two different days should end up with the same priorities. In order to ensure this, there must be a master list somewhere with the priority of standard tasks predetermined. Obviously, this master list will not be very large to start with. However, over time, this list can be added to and the priorities kept up to date. This is also not inviolable—the master list priorities may be overridden when needed. The overrides must be an exception and not a regular occurrence. When can the exception be exercised? There must be an objective basis and a rigorous process for overriding priorities. Otherwise, there is no value in creating the master list and prioritizing the items.

The A-1 method

This is a simple prioritization technique attributed to Alan Lakein. He described it first in his now classic *How to Get Control of Your Time and Your Life*. Alan Lakein is often considered the father of modern time management. He formulated the most important question in time management, "What is the best use of my time right now?" In his honor, this question is now called the **Lakein Question**.

In the A-1 method, the items in the task list must be first classified under A (most important) tasks, B (less important) tasks, and C (least important) tasks. The tasks within each category must be assigned priority numbers where 1 is the highest priority and higher numbers have successively lower priority. Thus, A-1 is the highest priority task among the most important ones. It is the first task that must be done, hence the name of the method. After each task is completed, the next in priority (A-2) will be selected, and so on down the line. If, while working on a particular task, another task is added to the master list or the classification or priority of any other tasks on the list has been modified, the list must be re-ordered before the next task is selected. This ensures that the next task selected is indeed the most important and highest in priority.

The question to consider at this stage is: where are the lines that divide the A tasks from the B tasks and the B tasks from the C tasks? I have a different way of looking at the A, B, and C categories. I consider A tasks as those that *must* be done (mandatory), B tasks are those that *may* be done (optional) if time permits, and C tasks are those that *would be nice* to get done (wish list).

Importance and urgency

Dwight D. Eisenhower was the 34th president of the United States of America from 1953 to 1961. Before that, he had been a general in the United States Army and had served as the Allied Forces Supreme Commander during World War II. He later also became the first NATO Supreme Commander. As busy as he was, he created a very simple evaluation technique to determine what he would focus on next.

When confronted with something that needed to be done, he asked only two questions: first, is this important? Secondly, is this urgent? The answers to the questions put the task in one of four categories:

- **Urgent** and **Important**: Crises and deadline-driven tasks
- **Important** but **Not Urgent**: Strategic planning, prospecting, and building relationships
- **Urgent** but **Not Important**: Interruptions and drop-in visitors
- **Not Important** and **Not Urgent**: Busy work and time wasters

The Eisenhower Matrix was rediscovered and popularized by Dr. Stephen Covey in his books *The 7 Habits of Highly Effective People* and *First Things First*. They are also called the **Covey Quadrants**.

Dr. Covey recommended that we must try to work mostly on Quadrant II (Important but Not Urgent) tasks. Quadrants III and IV contain the unimportant tasks. There is no value received from accomplishing these tasks. We usually approach Quadrant I (Urgent and Important) tasks in a reactive manner. These are usually unexpected and there is usually no time to think things through. The best that we can do is slap together a temporary solution and wait to find a proper solution. As I often say, you cannot perform brain surgery in the emergency room. Quadrant II tasks, however, give us ample opportunity to think things through and formulate a complete solutions. We can be proactive. That is the value of Quadrant II.

	Urgent	Not Urgent
Important	I ACTIVITIES: Crises Pressing problems Deadline-driven projects	II ACTIVITIES: Prevention Relationship building Recreation New opportunities
Not Important	III ACTIVITIES: Interruptions Some phone calls Some mail Some meetings Popular activities	IV ACTIVITIES: Trivia Some mail Some phone calls Time wasters Pleasure activities

How do you determine whether something is important? Is there a line that divides the important tasks from the unimportant or is it more like a broad band? Is it black and white or are there shades of gray? For the purpose of prioritization, I prefer a clear determination, that is, a sharp line and not a broad band. As I mentioned earlier, I recommend the use of a predetermined master list with relative ranks of different kinds of tasks. This only determines whether something is more or less important than something else. However, if one task is set as the benchmark of importance, everything above that point (inclusive of the benchmark) can be put in the first two quadrants, and everything else can be put in the last quadrants. This allows the students to have an objective and consistent way of putting tasks into appropriate lists.

How do you determine whether something is urgent? This determination is more objective. Something is urgent if:

> **The task demands immediate attention**: For example, the ringing telephone and screaming ambulance siren demand immediate attention. They are urgent but not necessarily important. In the past, it was necessary to pick up the phone to find out who was calling, but with the modern convenience of caller ID, incoming telephone calls can be screened.

> **The task is expected to be completed already or in the immediate future**: For example, on the day before the deadline to file tax returns, the task is expected to be done within the allotted time.

> **The task will take more time to complete than available**: For example, a project that would ordinarily take a month to complete becomes an urgent task when only three weeks are available.

Having objective criteria to evaluate subjective situations allows one to be consistent while making decisions.

Exercises

The exercises in this section build upon the previous work done in this chapter.

First, discuss the kinds of tasks that would go into the A, B, and C categories in the A-1 method and the four quadrants in the Eisenhower Matrix or Covey Quadrants. This discussion would drive home the points about relative importance, mandatory and optional tasks, and urgency. Another point in this discussion will lead to the next section about filtering tasks: what tasks are not important? Quadrants III and IV contain such tasks. When these are identified in discussion, it will be easy to drive home the concepts of deleting or delegating tasks.

The next part of the exercise is to take the activity list from the previous exercise and classify the tasks using both A-1 Method and the Urgent/Important quadrants.

Filtering tasks

Now that we have gone over how to identify the urgency and importance of tasks and put forth prioritization strategies, there is a temptation to delete the unimportant tasks and focus only on the important ones. Is this good enough? What is not important to one person may be a critical game-changer for someone else. Is it fair to delete something just because it is not important enough for you to work on?

The 4 Ds

The 4 Ds is a classic task filtration process. It stands for *Delete, Do, Delegate, Defer*. These are the four things that you can do with any task. Obviously, when some tasks are deleted, some delegated, and some deferred, considerably fewer tasks will remain to be done.

Let's see how this relates to the prioritization steps.

Quadrant IV tasks (Not Important, Not Urgent) and Quadrant III tasks (Not Important but Urgent) may be deleted **except** if the task is important to someone else. If it is important enough to someone else, it may be delegated.

Make a note

A sidebar about delegation

There are two important points that everyone should know about delegation—what to delegate and whom to delegate to. It is not only the tasks that are not important (Quadrants III and IV) that must be delegated if not deleted.

Consider a SWOT chart:

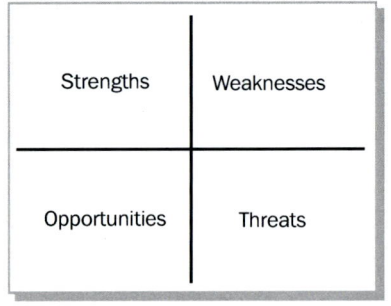

Strengths	Weaknesses
Opportunities	Threats

This is a great tool for understanding the internal picture (strengths and weaknesses) and the external picture (opportunities and threats), as well as looking at the positives (strengths and opportunities) and the negatives (weaknesses and threats). We are supposed to use our strengths in order to exploit opportunities and recognize our weaknesses in order to face up to and neutralize threats. I have heard it said that we should expand the strengths column by working on some of the weaknesses and converting them to strengths. I beg to differ. When we work on our weaknesses, we lose the opportunity to improve our strengths. We will never be strong enough to completely convert a weakness to a strength. After all the effort, all we will have are stronger weaknesses and weaker strengths. I recommend that we should work on our strengths and *delegate* weaknesses to someone else's strengths.

> **Make a note**
>
> Now to answer the questions about delegation.
>
> What do we delegate? We delegate tasks that are not important to us but important to someone else, and tasks that we are not strong in, that is, tasks that expose our weaknesses. Before we look to delegate a task, we must first determine whether the task *can* be delegated. The task may not be important to us but we may be important to the task! For example, if a contract cannot be accepted unless a key person verifies, validates, and approves it, the key person cannot delegate the task.
>
> Whom do we delegate to? We delegate tasks to someone who is strong in that area.
>
> One final point about delegation: I stated previously that when we hand over a task to someone else, we lose control over the process. We must trust that the task will be done to the best of that person's ability. It behooves us to follow up and track the progress, but it defeats every purpose of delegation when we micromanage the process! Trust that it will be done and let go.

In the Eisenhower Matrix (or Covey Quadrants), Quadrants I and II contain important tasks. Of these, if there are any urgent tasks, that is, Quadrant I (Important and Urgent), we must defer the non-urgent tasks that is, Quadrant II (Important but Not Urgent), and work on the urgent ones. Otherwise, if there are no urgent tasks, we can work on the non-urgent tasks. Dr. Stephen Covey recommended that we spend most of our time working on Quadrant II tasks because such tasks allow us to be proactive. We are generally reactive when working on Quadrant I tasks.

Where is the line that divides Quadrant I and Quadrant II? When does a task go from being non-urgent to being urgent? There is no absolute line. There is only a feeling that comes from experience.

Another way to apply the four Ds to the four quadrants may be: delete Quadrant IV tasks (neither Important nor Urgent), delegate Quadrant III tasks (Urgent but not Important), defer Quadrant II tasks (Important but not Urgent), and do the rest, that is, Quadrant I (Important and Urgent) tasks.

We can use a similar consideration for the A-1 Method. We can delete the C tasks. Of the As and Bs, we can delegate those tasks wherein we are not the key people, defer the tasks that are not pressing, and do the rest.

The Pareto Principle

Another filter that we may explore is the Pareto Principle. Developed by business management consultant Joseph Juran based on the observations of the Italian economist Vilfredo Pareto, the Pareto Principle states that 80% of the effects come from 20% of the causes.

In sales, this is stated as "80% of sales come from 20% of the clients."

In time management, 20% of the tasks provide 80% of the value. Since this principle is based on the results and not the effort, it is necessary to track the benefit of tasks for a period of time, say about three weeks, before we can apply this filter. That said, this is a very powerful filter because it maximizes the value we can realize from time.

Exercises

There are four exercises in this section.

The first is a discussion about tasks that may be delegated. Most people ask the question "Is this task important to me?" Not many address the question, "Am I important to this task?" Exploring these questions really drive home the ideas about what may be delegated, what must be delegate, and what may not be delegated.

The second exercise is a discussion about tasks that may be deleted. Again, people address the question, "Is this task important to me?" Not many consider whether the task is important to anyone else. This discussion opens up the students to different points of view and to value the opinions of others.

The third exercise is to work with the output of the previous set of exercises and apply filters to the prioritized lists created earlier. The value of this exercise is that it shows them how much time may be saved through the filtration process.

The final exercise in this section is to discuss the Pareto Principle as it applies to time management. Many students may be familiar with this principle but not with the fact that it applies to time management.

Task dependencies

Many tasks do not exist by themselves, especially in corporate environments and team-oriented work. These tasks are part of task sequences such as projects, processes, and operations. (For the purpose of this training material, I use the term *task sequence* to denote a project, a process, an operation, or any path thereof.) They may begin only when other tasks are complete and certain conditions are met. They depend on other tasks for information and collaboration.

There are two kinds of dependencies. For the purpose of this training material, I will call them *internal* and *external* dependencies. If all the tasks in a task sequence are performed by the same individual or members of a close-knit team, these tasks have internal dependencies only. If any task in a task sequence is performed by someone outside of the close-knit team, the tasks have external dependencies. This definition is only to show that we have control over internal dependencies but no control or very limited control over external dependencies.

Dependencies play a significant role in determining the next task to be selected. A task that may have been put into Quadrant II may suddenly get escalated to Quadrant I because of a dependent task. Dependencies are generally handled well in project plans but not as well in processes and operations.

The best strategy to handle the dynamics of dependent tasks is to identify and monitor dependencies, track upstream tasks that may disrupt schedules, and build in safeguards in our current tasks.

Exercise

The only exercise in this section is a discussion: what is the impact of dependencies on a schedule, especially prioritization?

Summary

Task management is one of the core processes in time management. This answers the key question, "What is the best use of my time right now?"

In order to answer this question, we need to identify the various demands on our time, make a list of tasks, prioritize the tasks, filter the list of tasks, and act on the remaining tasks.

The demands on our time stem from the various roles we have in our personal and professional lives. They can also be classified under routine tasks, required tasks, optional tasks, obligatory tasks, desired tasks, and goal-oriented tasks. By thinking of the various roles and goals within each role, we could come up with quite a large list of tasks that need to get done.

After the lists are made, we must prioritize the tasks according to importance and urgency. Tasks fall into four classes or quadrants: Quadrant I (Urgent and Important), Quadrant II (Important but Not Urgent), Quadrant III (Urgent but Not Important), and Quadrant IV (Neither Important Nor Urgent). Tasks can also be prioritized according to most important, less important, and least important or must do, may do, and would like to do.

After tasks are prioritized, they may be filtered using the 4 Ds—delete unimportant tasks, delegate tasks that are better done by others, defer tasks that are not urgent, and do the rest. Another filter is the Pareto Principle, which states that 20% of the tasks give you 80% of the value. By identifying the value of the tasks over a period of time, we can eliminate the 80% of tasks that only yield 20% value.

Finally, since many tasks do not exist alone but as a part of task sequences (projects, processes, and operations), they are subject to dependencies. Dependencies change the dynamics of tasks since they change priorities and can quickly change the urgency of downstream tasks. It is important to identify and monitor dependencies in order to prevent, avoid, and recover from unexpected demands on time.

In the next chapter, we will see the next important process in time management, schedule management. This includes keeping track of meetings and appointments so that we can be where we are supposed to at the time that we are expected to be there.

>4
Schedule Management

In this chapter, we will address punctuality, a quality that is respected and valued. This is the most visible benefit of time management. When people consistently show up where they are expected to be at the expected time, they are considered to be not only punctual but also *reliable* and *responsible*. Punctuality is not difficult to achieve. It only requires two sets of actions, **schedule management** and **schedule compliance**. Schedule management involves keeping track of all appointments and meetings, that is, all activities that show up on the calendar. Schedule compliance involves taking action to ensure that the schedule is observed, including closing all current activities and traveling towards the rendezvous point.

Here is an important distinction between tasks and schedules—tasks are intrapersonal and schedules are interpersonal. Tasks are undertaken at an individual level (many tasks that require group or team effort still have individual components) and appointments or meetings involve more than one person. This distinction is what makes schedule management significant—it affects other people. In other words, when you do not manage your tasks well, it only affects your time; when you do not manage appointments and meetings well, it affects your time and the time of all those who are part of that meeting or appointment. If you do not manage time well while working upon a task, you are wasting your own time. If you do not arrive punctually to appointments and meetings, you are wasting the time of all those who have arrived on time. When you are punctual, you indicate that you respect the other person's time. This is why punctuality is associated with responsibility, reliability, and dependability.

Both schedule management and deadline management (*Chapter 6, Deadline Management*) deal with keeping promises. Schedule management is a skill that helps us *be somewhere* at or before a specified time. Deadline management lets us *do something* at or before a specified time.

In both cases, expectations are being met. The key to both, therefore, is the ability to manage expectations. Promise only what can be delivered, and deliver on promises. When making an appointment, setting or accepting a meeting, or agreeing to complete a task within a specific timeframe, we must make sure that we can, indeed, keep the appointment, attend the meeting or complete the task as promised. Having made the promise, it behooves us to act in a manner such that we keep the promise.

How we handle deadlines is discussed in a later chapter. This chapter focuses on meetings and appointments.

Definitions

Before we go further in this section, let's properly set the context. It is necessary to lay down some definitions: what is the difference between an appointment and a meeting?

According to several dictionaries including the Oxford English Dictionary and the Merriam-Webster Dictionary, an appointment is an agreement to meet with someone at a certain place and time, and a meeting is a gathering or assembly of people, especially members of a society or committee, for a particular purpose such as discussion, entertainment, or worship.

For the purpose of this document:

- An **appointment** is defined as:
    - An agreement between a few individuals to meet for a definite purpose at a certain place at a specified date and time. It is a one-time arrangement. It is likely that the subject is more significant to one group of attendees than any other.
    - Alternatively, an agreement with a professional in order to avail his or her services at a specific place, usually the premises where the professional normally conducts business, at a specific date and time. This need not be a one-time encounter: depending on the profession and the nature of the services, the appointments may be quite frequent.
- A **meeting** is defined as a gathering of individuals for a common purpose at a certain place at a specified date and time.

Both appointments and meetings have:

- **Purpose**: Addressing the question "Why?"; one or more issues to consider and resolve
- **Participants**: Addressing the question "Who?"; two or more individuals whose input is required to achieve the stated purpose
- **Location**: Addressing the question "Where?"; a place that is suitable for the purpose
- **Date and time**: Addressing the question "When?"; everyone involved must be available to come together for the purpose at the same time

Why is this important? How does knowing the difference between appointments and meetings impact time management especially for new employees? There are differences in the way appointments and meetings are made, maintained, prepared for, acted upon, and followed-up on afterwards. Knowing the differences helps us act in an efficient manner.

The following sections cover how we make, maintain, prepare for, act upon, and follow-up on appointments and meetings. The common points are stressed and the differences are discussed.

Now that we have a common frame of reference as to what appointments are, let's explore their management.

There are five stages in the life of an appointment or a meeting: creation, maintenance, preparation, encounter, and follow-up. Not all appointments and meetings pass through all five stages. For example, maintenance may result in the cancellation of the appointment or meeting thus eliminating the encounter and follow-up stages. Some appointments and meetings do not require a follow-up, and others do not require maintenance. At the minimum, all appointments and meetings are created (that is, calendar entries are made), and appointments and meetings that are not cancelled result in an encounter. Any preparation required precedes the encounter but only if not cancelled.

Exercise

The only exercise in this section is to make a list of regular (periodic) meetings you attend and to verify that the meetings have the properties listed previously (purpose, participants, location, and date/time).

Handling appointments

As mentioned earlier, an appointment is an agreement between several individuals to rendezvous at a specific location at a specific date and time to discuss a specific issue. For there to be an agreement between several individuals, everyone concerned must be available at the same time. Availability is not the only criterion—if it were so, the number of appointments every individual schedules would grow exponentially! An appointment is a demand on an individual's time, and, as such, all demands on a person's time must be evaluated objectively:

> Is it *important* enough to warrant spending time on? In fact, is it important enough to dislodge another meeting if needed?

> Can this be delegated? Am I the only person who can contribute to this issue or can anyone else act in my stead?

> Is it convenient to attend? If not, will the benefits outweigh the inconvenience?

> Will this align with values, goals, and intermediate steps?

In the beginning, new employees will attend meetings and keep appointments because they have been asked to do so by their managers. It is still useful to answer the previous questions in order to get into the habit of thinking in these terms so that when they are in a position to make these decisions, they will have the tools to be able to do so.

Creating the appointment involves blocking the time on the calendar—paper or electronic—and filling in the details, namely, what, why, where, who, and when. We must first verify that the time is available not only to keep the appointment but also to get there in time from the previous activity. If other appointments are affected by the creation of this one, they must be modified upon discussion with the people affected.

One does not merely attend meetings and appointments. Many meetings and appointments depend on actions performed or information obtained prior to the meeting. Creating the appointment is a trigger to begin the preparatory work. Indeed, an appointment is an agreement. While not binding in the legal sense of the word, it is still a contract that an individual is obliged to perform towards. Therefore, before creating an appointment merely on the basis of availability and convenience, one must consider whether he or she is able and willing to perform all the tasks required in preparation for the appointment.

Maintaining appointments

There are two kinds of actions that may be taken in order to maintain appointments—modification and cancellation. Modification includes changing aspects of the appointment including purpose, location, attendees, date, and time. Modification requires the same considerations as creation—availability, convenience, relevance, importance, alignment with goals, and whether it can be delegated. Cancellation indicates that the purpose is no longer relevant, that is, the issue has been resolved, or the time or place is no longer available or convenient.

The need to modify or cancel the appointment may arise from any of the individuals involved. The request must be created and handled professionally, that is, the language must be appropriate. For example, if you need to request change of date, time, or location, do account for the fact that the previous date, time, or location was the result of discussion and agreement. Therefore, do recognize and commiserate with the inconvenience that the other(s) is (are) put to when you request the change. It must be a request, not a demand.

Preparing for an appointment

Many years ago, I was an assistant to a person who evaluated certain petitions and made recommendations based on his evaluation. While he was a very fair and objective person, he carefully recorded all his observations and analysis that justified his recommendations. He lived by an interesting credo: justice must not only be done, it must also *appear* to have been done. Appearance, in his opinion, was as important as the outcome.

Good schedule management results in the appearance of punctuality, reliability, responsibility, and professionalism. Good preparation boosts this image.

There are three aspects of preparation that we can consider:

> **Pre-appointment actions and information:** Is there a report that must be prepared and disseminated to all attendees? Is there any data that must be analyzed prior to the appointment?

> **Alarms and reminders:** An alarm may be set to get one started depending on how long it would take to get to the rendezvous point from the current location. Block out travel time to and from appointments to ensure punctuality.

> **Wait time actions:** When was the last time you saw the doctor without waiting in the little room outside, or without waiting in the examination room? When was the last time a meeting started and ended exactly on time? There is always some time spent in waiting for all the attendees to arrive and settle down. One of the biggest time wasters is wait time. Most people can waste hours but cannot wait even minutes. When they are forced to do nothing, that is when they realize how much work there is to be done and what they could have done in the little time they waited. One way to prepare for this is to anticipate the need—essentially, expect that *every* meeting will involve at least a short delay—and carry something along that can be done while waiting. This could be routine paperwork or other mindless activity.

The appointment

When the appointment does get under way, it is important to focus on the purpose of the meeting and move it firmly yet gently along.

There are several ways that meetings could get sidetracked:

> **Some people ramble on interminably:** When the matter being spouted is not relevant to the meeting (even it is relevant to the people at the meeting), it is necessary to cut in and either request that the point be discussed offline, that is, outside the meeting, or to create another meeting to discuss that point.

> **Some people air their grievances:** Again, even if the point is relevant to the people at the meeting, if it is not on the agenda, request to discuss the point offline or create another meeting to discuss that point.

> **Some people take every opportunity to advance their political agenda:** There are those who use every situation to point out how they had maintained a certain position, advanced a certain argument, operated in a certain capacity, and so on. If these are not relevant to the agenda item under discussion, they may be taken offline or in a different meeting.

> **Some people hold sidebar conversations:** Some people have conversations with their neighbors at meetings while someone else has the floor. Such sidebars are distracting and disruptive. Meeting etiquette must be maintained.

> **There are those who get sidetracked quite easily:** This is called the BSO syndrome—to be attracted to the bright, shiny object that flits by. With people who have no control over their attention, it is necessary for another individual to take responsibility for keeping them on the main track.

Since time, the limited resource, has been set aside for the purpose of the appointment to the exclusion of everything else, it is prudent and economical to keep everyone's attention on the agreed purpose of the meeting.

Even if you are not in control of the meeting, it is in your interest—and in the interest of all attendees—to work with the person in charge of the meeting to stick to the agenda and to move the meeting along. Very often, there is a designated timekeeper with enough authority to call the meeting back to order, take nagging items offline, curtail sidetracking, and so on.

Follow-up

As the appointment proceeds, things may come up that require further information or action and get assigned to the various attendees. Follow-up involves ensuring that all the information is gathered and all the actions are completed. Follow-up may also require further appointments to be set up. Again, it is a mark of responsibility and professionalism to follow through on commitments and follow-up on open items to bring them to closure. An effective follow-up is important in terms of time management as it ensures that your time already spent hasn't been wasted—not to mention the time you spend trying to put things right later.

Exercise

The first exercise in this section of the chapter is to validate the four phases of appointments. Are there any more phases? Can things be done differently? For clarity, analyze past appointments and see what went right, what went wrong, and what could have been managed using the concepts of appointment management.

For the next exercise identify a future appointment and ensure that the questions of what, why, where, who, and when are answered. You should then identify pre-appointment tasks and list them so as to prepare for the appointment.

Meetings

The primary difference between appointments and meetings is in the way they are managed. Appointments flow more or less according to the whims of the more powerful person—generally less affected by the purpose of the meeting. Meetings are supposed to be run according to an *agenda*. Before discussing agendas, let's quickly go over something common between meetings and appointments—maintenance. Meetings, too, may be moved or cancelled. It is important to communicate such changes to all invitees so that they do not unnecessarily end up attending a meeting that no longer exists or go to the wrong place or attend at the wrong time. In fact, good communication is very critical to effective meeting management.

Agenda

An agenda is a list of items to be discussed at a formal meeting. As each item is resolved, the meeting moves on to the next item. In fact, most meetings begin with an agreement on the agenda.

An agenda can be used to determine the meeting invitees. The host or organizer should only invite those individuals to whom the agenda is relevant and who can contribute to the resolution of one or more items on the agenda. The invitees, too, can determine their own contribution to the meeting based on the published agenda and decide whether or not to accept the invitation.

A well-run meeting has the following structure:

> **Introduction**: The overarching purpose of the meeting is introduced, followed by the introduction of attendees.

> **Agenda Items**: Each item on the agenda is discussed for a specific duration. The duration is controlled so that the discussions do not become open-ended. The meeting is set for a limited amount of time. Only by controlling the time spent on individual agenda items can all items be discussed. Each item is either resolved or tabled for resolution at a subsequent meeting. Action items that come out of the resolution are assigned to individuals with a time limit for the action.

> **Summary**: The discussion is summed up, resolutions restated, action items and the assignments thereof are confirmed, and the time for each follow-up action is clearly defined.

In general, the introduction should take no more than the first five minutes of the meeting and the summary the last five. The remaining time may be divided equitably between the agenda items.

Agenda item resolution

Each item on the agenda must be introduced and discussed, resolved, or explored further. Some items, for example, routine activities, need not be discussed in depth but merely assigned to someone. New items and significant issues may require more information and discussion. If necessary, items may be moved to another meeting to give it additional time or assigned to a subgroup for further discussion.

The discussion about each agenda item must, therefore, result in:

> **Resolution**: The issue is solved and the solution must be shared with relevant individuals.

> **Assigned**: The issue will be resolved by an action. The action is assigned to an individual and a time limit set on the assignment.

> **Deferred**: The issue needs to be discussed some more. A new meeting is created to give the issue the time required.

> **Delegated**: A subgroup is created to solve the issue. The person responsible for the solution is identified and a time limit set on the assignment.

Meeting minutes

Meeting minutes are the record of a meeting or hearing. They record the attendees, the agenda, points raised during the discussion, the resolution of agenda items, the person assigned the action or the responsibility of the subgroup, and deadline for the response. They serve as a reference to resolve future discussions.

The following template can be created in Microsoft Excel. The contents in regular font are defined prior to the meeting. The contents in italics are discovered during the meeting. While the meeting is in session, one person must be assigned the task of capturing the meeting minutes and filling out the changing content. In this manner, the minutes will be created almost as soon as the meeting is complete.

The use of this template as a meeting management guide will ensure that meetings do not go out of control and do complete on time.

		Meeting Agenda and Minutes Template			
Purpose:					
Invitees:		*Attended*			
	John	*No*			
	Jane	*Yes*			
	Thomas	*Yes*			
	Richard	*Yes*			
	Harriet	*No*			
Agenda	*Arguments*	*Resolution*	*Action Item*	*Assigned to*	*Deadline*

Exercises

The first exercise is to understand the use of an agenda to drive a meeting. Is an agenda necessary? Is it valuable? What is the value of an agenda? How does it relate to time management? An agenda is to a meeting what a checklist is to a pilot when the plane takes off or lands. Items on the agenda must be addressed and completed before moving on. Paper remembers what the mind forgets. By having a list of actionable items, you ensure that the purpose of the meeting is served.

The second exercise is to analyze a prior meeting. Were the attendees relevant to the discussion? Was the discussion relevant to the attendees? What was the agenda? Was the agenda followed? Were the items on the agenda resolved? Were there actions assigned to specific people? Were definite time limits set on the actions? Did the meeting begin on time and complete on time?

The last exercise is to go through the process of recording meeting minutes for a quick meeting. The exercise allows you to understand the process of driving meetings through agendas and also a quick way of tracking minutes.

Summary

Schedule management is another key process in time management. While tasks are pertinent to an individual, meetings and appointments involve other people. This is why punctuality is valued—punctuality proves that one is reliable, responsible and values other peoples' time.

Appointments go through four phases—creation, maintenance, encounter, and follow-up. Creation is based not only on availability, that is, whether we are available at a specific point in time, but also on relevance and convenience. Maintenance includes deleting the appointment (no longer relevant) and changing aspects of the appointment (who, where, and when). As an appointment is an agreement to come together, it must be treated as a contract and respected as such.

Meetings also must be maintained as appropriate. While appointments are run according to the whim of the more powerful party in the gathering, meetings must be run according to an agenda, that is, a list of items to be discussed at the meeting. The agenda also determines who should be invited based on relevance and who can contribute to the discussion about the items on the agenda. The agenda should also be used as a guideline for the invitees to use to accept or reject the invitation.

The items on the agenda must be introduced, discussed, resolved, or assigned to individuals for resolution. When assigned, there must be a definite time limit set so to ensure that the task gets completed.

Meeting minutes are used to record the proceedings of meetings. They are used to keep track of attendees, agenda, resolution, or assignment and deadlines. Meeting minutes can be quickly created by the use of a template.

The topic has many concepts to explore and discuss. The first point is the value of punctuality. It is important to recognize how valuable time is to other people. It is one thing to waste one's own time; wasting other people's time indicates a callous and selfish attitude.

The second point is the distinction between appointments and meetings. While this may feel like semantics, it is important to create a common set of terms in order to have common processes and expectation. Appointments and meetings share common attributes and differ in composition, purpose, and the way in which they are managed. Is this a useful distinction?

Schedule Management

The third concept is the use of paper or electronic schedule management tools. Meetings and appointments must be tracked on some kind of calendar management tool in order to find available time and to avoid clashes, that is, to avoid scheduling two events at the same time. How else may calendars be used?

The fourth concept is the management of appointments. The four phases—creation, maintenance, encounter, and follow-up—are a useful breakdown to control appointments. Are there other steps?

The last concept is the management of meetings. For this, we usually have two tools, agendas, and meeting minutes. However, they can be combined into a single tool. Is this useful? How have meetings been run in the past? Will the knowledge they glean from this session help them manage meetings better?

In the next chapter, we will delve deeper into managing daily tasks. This activity takes the master task list created by identifying tasks and pruning the list by deleting some tasks and delegating others and brings the list into current context: how long will the tasks take, how much time is available for working on tasks, and, therefore, how much can be done given the available time? This process allows you to create a realistic daily task list.

> 5
Managing Daily Tasks

In this chapter, we will discover how to manage the daily task list. In other words, this is activity management in action. It is important to know what can be realistically achieved in a reasonable amount of time. This chapter explains how we can manage and meet expectations.

The activity list (from *Chapter 3, Task Management*) contains all the tasks that were identified and not rejected, that is, the tasks that survived the filtration process. This list indicates *what* must be done but not *when*. Can all the tasks on the activity list be done within the time available today? Or, more relevant to many people, is it *reasonable* to expect to complete all the tasks on the activity list today? This chapter will show how to select tasks from the activity list and create a list of tasks that can be reasonably expected to be completed in a day.

There are three principal concepts covered in this chapter:

- **Managing expectations**: What can be done within the available time.
- **Estimation**: How long a certain task will take.
- **Application**: How to create a realistic daily task list.

The value of these concepts cannot be stressed enough. When we manage expectations (that is, set and meet expectations), we protect our image and reputation. When we create and successfully execute an action plan for a day, we gain control over the events in life. Therefore, the concepts covered in this chapter go beyond their immediate application in the area of time management.

Managing expectations

Until Sir Roger Bannister did so on May 6, 1954 at Iffley Road Track in Oxford, everyone believed that it was impossible for a human being to run a mile in less than 4 minutes (Bannister did it in 3 minutes and 59.4 seconds). In other words, the *expectation* that someone could run a mile in under 4 minutes was considered *3*. Now, running a mile in under 3 minutes may be considered unrealistic until human endurance and ability increases to that level.

People deal with unrealistic expectations every day. I have heard many people tell me that time management as they knew it—making lists of tasks—did not work for them because they hardly completed a small fraction of the items on their lists and finally stopped the practice altogether. The problem was not that they did not complete the tasks; it was that they put more on their lists than they had any chance of completing.

In the earlier chapters, we discussed *creation* and *prioritization* of task lists. This includes filters to *delete* unnecessary tasks, *delegate* tasks that could be given to others, and *defer* tasks that are not urgent. However, it does not follow that the tasks that pass the filter must all be added to the current day's task list. Time is indeed a limited resource. There is only so much that can be done in the time that is available. It is not realistic to expect to do everything that remains on the prioritized and filtered list in the little time that we have after accounting for routine activities and required activities.

The dictionary defines the term "ration" as the "fixed allowance of provisions or food, especially for soldiers or sailors or for civilians during a shortage." Time, too, is a very scarce commodity: we ought to ration it in order to make do with this very scarce commodity.

How do we deal with a fixed allowance, whether of provisions, money, or time? If we had access to unlimited resources, there would be no restriction on how we put the resources to use. On the other hand, as the resources get limited, we restrict the use of the resources by priority. Likewise, the most important tasks get the first call upon our time, and the next important, and so on down the list.

Unrealistic expectations

What is the problem with unrealistic expectation? What is the result of overstuffing the daily task list?

When more is put on the daily task list than is reasonable, it will lead to:

> **Incomplete tasks and unmet expectations**: This will result in a poor image and reputation (external effect) and low self-esteem (internal effect).

> **Hurried attempts to complete everything at any cost**: This will result in poor quality of work (external effect) and a high level of stress (internal effect).

The point here is that it is not a good idea to try to do everything. It is important to recognize limits and abide by them. Anything else is unrealistic. A realistic expectation puts you in the right situation so that you stand a fair chance of completing what they set out to. As in anything else, success begets success in time management. When we are successful in meeting expectations, we tend to believe in the system and in our ability to use it. This will encourage you to stick to the practice.

Why do people attempt more than they can achieve?

There are three underlying causes:

- **Inability to say no**: Many people take on more tasks because they are unable to refuse. This may be because they feel it would be impolite or disrespectful to refuse, because of any obligation the requestor holds over them, or because they want to appear nice, helpful, or obliging. Imagine bailing out a boat that has a leak. If you are able to empty the boat faster than the intake from the leak, you will remain afloat. If the water comes in faster than you are able to cope with, the boat will sink. So, too, will you be overwhelmed if you take on tasks faster than you are able to complete them and clear your slate. One solution, therefore, is to only take on tasks at the same rate that they get completed, that is, to match the intake to the outflow. This means that you must either improve your efficiency (outflow) or limit the rate at which you take on tasks (intake), or both. In other words, if you cannot say "No" to a request, you must be able to finish things faster. Otherwise, to continue the leaky boat analogy, you will sink.

- **Overconfidence**: More tasks are sometimes added to the daily task list with the misplaced confidence that the tasks are trivial and could easily be done. Many seemingly easy tasks do take much longer than anticipated. This is either the result of not fully grasping all that the task entails, that is, not thinking things through, or a greater belief in one's own abilities than warranted, that is, hubris. The solution is to force you to think things through and understand everything that the task requires so as to have a better notion as to how long the task will take, that is, estimation.

- **Difficulty letting go**: Many tasks ultimately land up on an already overflowing daily task list because it is assumed that no one else can do the tasks. Many people are ineffective at delegation, and when they do delegate, they become micromanagers from hell. In the note *The sidebar on delegation* in *Chapter 3, Task Management*, we determined that we must delegate tasks that are not important to us but important to someone else, and tasks that we are not strong in, that is, tasks that expose our weaknesses. We also noted that we delegate the tasks to someone who is strong in that area. It is important to understand that a) delegation reduces the demand on our time and b) true delegation requires letting go. The solution, if it can be called a solution, is to focus on the more important things that don't get done by not letting go, that is, the benefits of delegation.

Here is an image that can quite succinctly illustrate the problem:

The knock-out punch

It is quite easy and natural to be overwhelmed by a pile of work that grows out of control. It is important to limit the workload to one's capability. While this can be termed as the workload capacity from your personal viewpoint, it has to be portrayed to those who assign work to you as your workload limit so as to have an objective reason to avoid overloading.

The problem of unrealistic expectations—too much work, not enough time—can also be related to attempting to overfill a balloon (BOOM!) or the water pressure building up behind a dam. As humans, we can only do so much and must realize this truth.

The concept of managing expectations is quite abstract. There are two aspects of this concept: *managing what others expect of us* and *managing what we expect of ourselves*. The former is important because by setting the bounds of what we can achieve and consistently staying within those bounds, we can make sure that no one asks us to achieve the impossible. By (slightly) under promising and (slightly) over delivering, we can build a healthy reputation. Managing our own expectations is harder and more important. What it reveals is our understanding of our capabilities.

Dealing with expectations efficiently

How can we manage expectations?

The solution is quite simple, really. There are three parts to this solution:

1. **Determine how much time is available for tasks**. This is done by summing up all the time that is committed (routine tasks, meetings and appointments, commute) and subtracting this sum from 24 hours. Do remember that one needs to eat and sleep!
2. **Estimate how much time each task will take**. This is described in detail in the next section. For now, realize that this is a finite amount of time and must be taken into consideration.
3. **Determine the tasks that can fit into the available time**. This, too, will be described in a subsequent section. For now, understand that this process will yield a consistent and objective behavior pattern.

This process gives us a clear idea about what can be realistically attempted or achieved in the given time. If the purpose is to manage our own expectations (internal), this result can be used to control our daily task list. If the purpose is to manage what others expect of us (external), this result must be effectively communicated to the entities that matter, for example, manager, peers, direct reports, board of directors, investors, and committees.

One last point about managing expectations: Promise only what can be delivered and deliver on promises. I prefer to actually under promise and slightly (about 10 percent) over deliver. When we meet and slightly exceed what others expect of us, we gather a very favorable reputation. This is a very valuable attitude to adopt.

By properly managing expectations:

- The daily task list will be brought under control
- The tendency to overstuff the list will be controlled
- There will be an objective reason to be able to say no and refuse more work
- There will be a greater awareness of capability and limitation
- Overconfidence will be tempered and balanced against ability
- The work done will be of great quality
- Stress will be reduced

The ultimate value of managing expectations is in the control one will have over activities, actions, and results.

The application of this concept, managing expectations, goes beyond creating realistic daily task lists. The generalized concept is:

- **Understand capability and limits thereof**: In the section on estimation that follows, I will show that an estimate reflects the complexity of a task and the ability to execute the task. Therefore, an accurate estimate indicates a good understanding of capability. Significant underestimation, that is, if the actual time to complete the task significantly exceeds the estimate, indicates limited ability and the need for improvement. Significant overestimation, that is, if the estimate significantly exceeds the actual time to complete the task, indicates great ability and available bandwidth. The first two cases, accurate estimate and underestimation, indicate the limits of capability.

- **Set expectations according to limits**: As mentioned earlier, the best way to manage expectations is to under promise and (slightly) over deliver. Overpromising is a problem as it leads to poor reputation. Significantly over delivering is also a problem because it sends the wrong signals. For example, many companies have service level agreements (SLAs) as to how quickly they will respond to and solve customer issues. If a company has a written agreement to respond and solve customer issues within 4 hours but consistently solves minor issues in 10 minutes, a major issue that requires the entire 4 hours to solve would leave the customer very dissatisfied. However, if the company deliberately sets expectations by solving even minor issues in nearly 4 hours, the customers are not upset if some issues really take 4 hours to solve.

- **Operate within the limits of capability (that is, do not attempt things that are clearly beyond capability)**: When you know the limits of capability, you will be encouraged to operate within those limits. For those who are loath to say "No", this knowledge provides reason and ammunition to do so.

- **Take steps to extend the limits of capability, for example, training or exercises**: Referring to the SWOT chart in *Chapter 3, Task Management*, if the skill is a "weakness", it can and should be delegated. However, if it can be improved, it should be in order to push the limits. Knowing the limits of various skills can enhance SWOT analysis to be able to make decisions as to which skills may be improved through training and practice and which must be delegated.

Exercise

The exercise in this section is to use the prioritized and filtered list developed through the exercises in *Chapter 3, Task Management*, and check if it would be reasonable to expect to complete all the tasks on the list in a day. The following is a quick process for this check:

1. Determine how much time is available for tasks given how much time is already committed to meetings and appointments.
2. Estimate how much time each task on the prioritized and filtered task list will take (a rough approximation will do for now: this exercise will be expanded later in this chapter with improved estimation techniques).

3. If the sum of the estimates is less than the time available, all the tasks on the list can be done (again, this is based on a rough approximation; better estimation techniques are explained in the following section).

Finally, although the solution at this point in time is only qualitatively described, ask them to discuss the benefits of managing expectations and whether they can see how the solution would yield the benefits.

Estimation

How long will it take to complete any task? It depends on two things—the task and the individual's prior experience with similar tasks.

Estimation may appear to be a very dry subject and overkill for trivial tasks. However, it is a very important step in managing expectations and creating realistic daily task lists.

An estimate is only a guess. Sometimes, it is an educated guess; sometimes, it is a calculated guess. In either case, it is still a guess. It becomes useful and effective when it is backed by plausible basis and reflects reality.

Any estimate could well be a number taken from thin air unless it is close to the actual time. An estimate can only be validated after the task is completed. A good estimate is within an acceptable range, for example, 5 percent or 10 percent of the actual duration of the task.

Why should we estimate how much time a task should take? For one, doing so helps us create realistic to-do lists. For another, it helps us see how well we are managing tasks. For example, if a task is completed in 15 minutes, is that good or bad? It depends. If the task was supposed (expected, estimated) to take 30 minutes and was completed in 15, it is good. However, if the task was supposed to take only 5 minutes and took 15, it is bad.

This is like asking if a net income of a million dollars is a good thing. It depends. If it took a billion dollars to generate a net income of a mere million dollars, that is terrible. However, if it took only half a million dollars to generate a net income of a million, that is terrific.

Let's look at three estimation models:

> **Historic average**
>
> How long has this task (or this type of task) taken in the past? If we know approximately how long it has taken on an average, that value is a good substitute for the estimate.
>
> As the name implies, this is not so much an estimate as it is a statistic. This model requires us to keep track of how long people have taken to complete the same task in the past. This model is only useful for repetitive tasks.

One limitation of this model is that different people may take quite different lengths of time to complete the same task. The estimate has to be adjusted for individual abilities.

Another limitation is that tasks do not scale well. If it takes an hour to paint two 12' X 15' walls, it will take more than 2 hours to paint four such walls. We need to account for fatigue and the need for breaks.

> **Expert opinion**

If you have not done something like this in the past, ask someone who has.

As the name implies, we merely defer to the opinion of an experienced person, an expert in the field. Given the parameters of the task, the expert pronounces a judgment as to how much time it should take to complete the task.

The limitation of this method is that it is a black box. We have no insight into the machinations that produce the estimate. We do not know if we need to adjust the estimate to account for the individual or if the estimate is scalable.

> **Divide and conquer**

In this method, the task is broken down into its constituent parts. Each part is estimated separately and the individual estimates are combined to form the whole estimate.

The whole is the sum of its parts. When you understand the parts, you understand the whole task. Another way of looking at this rule is to consider a path to the destination, and all intermediary points that must be passed in order to reach the target.

The limitation of this method is that at the lowest level, we must resort to historic average or expert opinion to get the estimate. However, this is the most flexible model since it allows for tasks not encountered previously: if the constituent parts can be estimated, the task can be estimated.

In order to accurately estimate how long a task should take, it is necessary to have complete information about the task. Task duration can be estimated even without complete information by:

1. Estimating the percentage of knowledge available.
2. Determining how the information translates to work.
3. Estimating the task based on available information.
4. Using the relationship between the information and the work as determined in *step 2* to expand the estimate in *step 3* to the entire task.

When you begin working with these estimation models, the main thing that you must appreciate is that one size does not fit all situations. You must select the most appropriate model or even mix and match models to get the best results. For example, when you have prior experience with similar tasks, you can use your historic average. Otherwise, you call an expert to get an idea as to how long the task should take. If what is being attempted has no previous models to compare against, the divide and conquer rule may be the best model to use.

The benefit of using estimation models to predict how long it will take to complete a task is that it allows us to get to the next stage, the creation of realistic daily task lists.

The interesting point here is that until recently, very few time management gurus recognized the need to estimate how long tasks would take. Therefore, very few time management systems addressed the issue of realism or setting realistic expectations. As a result, many students of time management courses were frustrated in their practice and gave up the use of planners and organizers. This leads me to believe that estimation is a key concept in time management.

The use of estimation not only allows the creation of realistic daily schedules, but it can also be used to promote efficiency. Doing something quickly does not mean that it cannot be done well. Only when something is done in a hurry or in a disorganized manner will quality suffer. The key word is *efficiency*. When something is done efficiently and expeditiously, it will be done right.

The time "saved" in executing a task efficiently is taken as the difference between the time the task was expected to take and the time the task actually took.

That is, *Time Saved = Estimate – Actual Duration.*

Therefore, one way of fomenting efficiency is to set a goal of always beating estimates. This will encourage you to embrace the culture of estimating how long every task will take.

If you do not have any expectation of how much time a task is supposed to take then you cannot know whether you completed the task efficiently or not. If you underestimate a task, odds are that you will not be able to beat the estimate and save time on that task. On the other hand, you can fool the system by always overestimating task durations, but that will bring down your productivity.

A *realistic* expectation puts you in the ballpark such that you stand a fair chance of at least meeting expectation. With a realistic expectation, even if you did under estimate, you would not grossly under estimate so much that you will be able to recover the lost time soon. And if you did over estimate, it would still not bring down your productivity.

As mentioned earlier in this chapter, people attempt more than they can achieve due to the inability to say "No", overconfidence and the inability to let go and delegate. Estimation is a good cure for the second problem, that is, overconfidence. A good estimate combines the complexity of the task with the individual's ability to complete the task. Indeed, just like in economics, the price of an item is the point where the demand for the item meets its supply, the estimate for a task can be perceived as the point where the complexity of the task meets ability.

Whether an estimate is a "good" estimate or not can only be determined after the task is completed. If an estimate is inaccurate, that is, if the actual time taken to complete the task differs from the estimate by a significant margin (for example, 15 percent or more), it means either that the complexity of the task is poorly understood or that the individual has an incorrect perception of his/her ability. Therefore, estimation is also an exercise for improving one's understanding of complexity and ability.

An estimate is very individual. While the second estimation method, expert opinion, gets input from an expert as to how long a task should take, that estimate should be normalized to an individual's experience or lack thereof. For example, nearly two decades ago, I decided to have two rooms in my home repainted. I called a painter for an estimate. He told me that he could coat the two rooms, including the ceilings, in 4 hours and would return the next day for a second coat of paint. Since I had a few days off, I decided to take on this project by myself. Inexperienced as I was, I took more than 12 hours for the first coat! The estimate of 4 hours assumed a certain level of ability and experience.

Creating a realistic daily tasks list

In this section, we shall repeat the previous exercise but with better estimates, that is, to take the rough approximations created in the previous exercise and improve them using the three estimation techniques above. This is an eye-opener for many individuals: many people tend to underestimate when using rough approximations. The scientific approach to estimation uncovers this tendency and helps bring it under control.

A realistic daily task list is one which has just enough tasks such that there is a fair chance of completing all of them by the end of the day. A realistic plan ensures that there is enough time available for the activities to be completed, and that only as many activities are planned as can fit the time available. This prevents both overstuffing of the list of activities and excessive idling.

How is a realistic daily task list created? From 24 hours, the length of a day, take away the usual sleep time, the time needed for routine tasks, and the time usually lost in commuting to work. This is the *baseline* available time. For example, if you sleep for 7 hours on an average and spend 1 hour in the morning getting ready for the day, if you spend 1/2 hour each way getting to and from work, if you spend 1 hour for lunch and 3 hours in the evening for dinner, personal work, quality time with the family, winding down and getting ready for bed, you are left with 11 hours for work and other chores. Your baseline available time (BAT) is 11 hours. Of this time, you may spend 8 hours at work and use the other 3 hours for the tasks on your personal list.

> ➤ From the baseline of available time calculated earlier, take away time for known appointments and mandatory activities. This should include "scheduled tasks" as described shortly. The remaining time is the time available for tasks. For example, if you know that you have a staff meeting for 1 hour every morning, project status meeting for 1 hour every afternoon, and a department-wide meeting for 1 hour every Friday afternoon, you are left with 5 hours' professional time on Fridays. Likewise, if you have an hour-long meeting at 11 am and another at 2 pm, you are left with 3 hours to get your work done on Friday.

Managing Daily Tasks

> ➤ The available time can then be allocated to tasks from the prioritized and filtered task list. As each task is transferred from the master list to the daily task list, reduce the available time by the expected duration of the task. Stop adding tasks when either there is no more available time or when the available time is not enough to accomplish any of the tasks on the list. For example, if you have to write a report (estimate: 1 hour), run a set of calculations (estimate: 45 minutes), contribute to a design document (estimate: 75 minutes), file expenses for a business trip (estimate: 30 minutes), you do not have time to complete all these tasks unless you take a short lunch break or move the filing of expenses to the next business day. This can also relate to the use of the 3 hours for your personal tasks. For example, you may have to pick up a parcel at the post office, drop off laundry, pick up groceries, and have the car washed. If each of these activities takes 45 minutes, you have enough time to complete them all. Otherwise, you will have to reschedule some to the next possible opportunity.

Tip
When is a task a "scheduled task"?

Some tasks must be done at a specific time. These tasks are not "appointments" or "meetings". For example, if you had to pick your child up from the after-school care provider, would you consider that an appointment or meeting?

Some tasks may be done only before or after a certain time. For example, if you need to send a package by one of the overnight carriers (UPS, FedEx, DHL, and so on), you must reach the office before it closes. If you drop off a roll of film at a 1-hour film-processing center, you can pick it up an hour later. It is convenient to treat time-bound tasks as scheduled tasks.

The value of a realistic task list is that it enables and encourages you to complete everything on the list. Since success begets success, this helps you to stick with the system, become more effective and efficient, and improves your self-confidence.

Other concepts covered in this book, for example, schedule management and deadline management, are tangibly time-oriented. When you schedule an appointment, you know where you need to be at a certain time on a certain date, whom you will be meeting with and for what purpose. When you work towards a deadline, you have a definite target to reach within a certain time. However, when you have a list of things to be done without true deadlines, unless you control the schedule and implementation, it may run away from you. Managing the daily task list requires proactive control and is the most critical part of time management. Many individuals who fail to manage time fail in this area.

Exercise

The first exercise in this section is to have the employees calculate their baseline available time.

The final exercise in this chapter is to create a reasonable daily task list for one day from the baseline available time, the prioritized and filtered task list, and scheduled meetings, appointments, and tasks. This extends the exercise in the previous section. You can use the example and template described previously in the three-step process to create the daily task list, to do so. The template is restated here:

1. **Calculate baseline available time (BAT)**: From 24 hours, take away time for sleep, morning routine, commute, lunch, evening routine, and dinner.
2. **Calculate available time (AT)**: From the BAT, take away time for known appointments and meetings.
3. **Fill available time**: From the prioritized task list, add tasks one-by-one to the daily list and reduce available time by the estimate for the task until no more tasks can be added.

Summary

In this chapter, we have dealt with the creation of reasonable daily task lists. The purpose of the activity is to manage expectations such that the individual is not overwhelmed by overstuffed task lists nor is given to excessive idling when there is work to be done. This is accomplished by estimating how long each individual task should take using several estimation models, determining how much time is available for tasks, and only adding tasks that can be accomplished within the available time.

In the next chapter, we will see how we can manage deadlines. The chapter describes three problems or obstacles to meeting deadlines and shows strategies to overcome these obstacles.

> 6
Deadline Management

In this chapter, we will take a look at what it takes to get things done on time. While managing appointments calendar management or schedule management ensures that you be somewhere at or before a certain time, managing deadlines ensures that you do something at or before a certain time. Deadline management deals with results, especially time sensitive ones.

The concepts covered in this chapter include three forces that come in the way of meeting deadlines—**Parkinson's Law**, **Murphy's Law**, and the **Student Syndrome**—and three strategies to overcome them. Two of these strategies address the human tendencies that delay either the start or the completion of tasks. The third strategy addresses how to identify possible points of failure and to avoid them or recover from them.

Parkinson's Law

Cyril Northcote Parkinson made the following observation in a humorous article he penned for the Economist magazine in November of 1955:

> *"Work expands so as to fill the time available for its completion."*

While the original intent of the statement—and related article and book—was to "explain" (satire) the inevitability of bureaucratic expansion, the statement is valid in almost all situations. This statement is now popularly referred to as **Parkinson's Law**.

Parkinson gave the following example in his original article in the Economist, November 1955:

> *"It is a commonplace observation that work expands so as to fill the time available for its completion. Thus, an elderly lady of leisure can spend an entire day in writing and dispatching a postcard to her niece at Bognor Regis. An hour will be spent in finding the postcard, another in hunting for spectacles, half-an-hour in a search for the address, an hour and a quarter in composition, and twenty minutes in deciding whether or not to take an umbrella when going to the pillar-box in the next street. The total effort which would occupy a busy man for three minutes all told may in this fashion leave another person prostrate after a day of doubt, anxiety and toil."*

It is also commonly observed that if you need to get something done, give it to a busy person. For example, if you allocate an hour to writing a status report, it will take an hour to do so. If you allocate three hours to writing the same report, it will take three hours to do the same amount of work.

Why?

While I have not found any satisfactory explanation for this phenomenon, it is my belief that the mind paces itself according to time available.

In an experiment, I gave someone five days to implement a task that he expected to do in three. One day later, I asked him to try to finish the task in a day less, that is, four days from when the task was started or three days from that point in time. He found it impossible to do so, even though the original estimate for the task was three days! On the other hand, when I asked someone to implement a task in less time than expected and later gave some additional time, the task was finished on time.

Details that would otherwise be dropped get added in when time is available. There is also the strange habit of tinkering—trying to improve the outcome—when time is available.

The real issue here is not the availability of time but the allocation of time, that is, how much time is set aside for the purpose of this task. What this means is that after accounting for routine activities and scheduled meetings, if you have three hours available for working on your list of tasks, the entire time is not going to be dedicated to any single task: you will distribute the available time between some or all of the tasks on the list. The amount of time that you allocate for any given task will depend on your guess as to how long you expect that task to take, as discussed in the chapter on daily tasks. To recapitulate, the *true* estimate depends on the historic average (that is, how long the task has taken in the past), expert opinion (that is, how long an expert thinks the task should take), and divide and conquer (that is, estimate the parts of the task and put them together). Many people also add a little extra to the estimate to allow for contingencies. However, according to Parkinson's Law, any time allocated to a task over and above the *true* estimate as to how much time the task *should* take is wasted. What this means is that if we allocate extra time to allow for contingencies, the extra time is consumed irrespective of contingencies.

For example, it is a standard practice to *pad* all estimates with a safety margin. The safety margin typically runs from 5 percent to 35 percent of the estimate. However, only three tasks in ten really need the safety margin, or *buffer* as it is often referred to. In other words, for about 70 percent of the tasks, there is no real need for a buffer. On the other hand, if we do not allocate extra time for any task, three in ten tasks will exceed the allocated time.

The unfortunate side to all this is that Parkinson's Law does not work in reverse. We cannot save time by allocating less time to every task, nor can we improve productivity by forcing everyone to complete tasks in less time than possible. It may be possible to get a temporary improvement in productivity by cracking the whip and applying pressure, but prolonged use of pressure leads to fatigue and poor quality.

Deadline Management

While the concept of Parkinson's Law is independent of other concepts covered so far, it is important to understand estimation, that is, setting expectations as to how long a task *should* take, in order to truly grasp the impact of this law. As it is stated, work expands so as to fill the time *available* for its completion. The time available, that is, the time allocated for the task, should align with expectation. Therefore, when the task is well estimated through the use of the techniques covered in the previous chapter, there should be little impact due to Parkinson's Law. Poor estimation leads to greater impact.

Parkinson's Law is best understood through experience. As much as we may try to explain the difference between estimated time and allocated time for tasks, the concept comes home when you actually try to do something within time limits. For example, use activities such as sorting beads of several colors, stacking piles of matchsticks, sorting a shuffled deck of cards into suits and in order within each suit and try to complete these activities within a time limit. To make it interesting, play with the time limit.

The obvious application of this concept is in protecting deadlines. Many people add a modest extra to estimates as a safety margin. Parkinson's Law ensures that the safety margin is also consumed. Statistically, only three in ten tasks really need the safety margin. Therefore, in order to protect 70 percent of tasks from lower productivity, it is better not to add safety margins to any task. What about the 30 percent that do need safety margins? I usually add a dummy task in my list with 30 percent of the total margin. When a task overshoots estimate, I "borrow" from the dummy task. This scheme works most of the time.

For example, let's take ten tasks that one could encounter in the workplace:

- Write a status report for tasks on hand
- Pull together data for a quick analysis
- Search the Internet for a competitor's view on an issue
- Look through customer purchase history to identify top 3 customers
- Review a proposal before submitting to a prospect
- Evaluate three potential solutions to a problem and pick the best option
- Tabulate expenses from a recent business trip and submit expense report
- Create a spreadsheet to track time that will be spent on a new project
- Fill out questionnaire on a new process planned to be implemented in the workplace
- Create new meeting according to the convenience of three senior managers

To make things simple, let's set the "true" estimate of every one of these tasks at 40 minutes. It should take 400 minutes, or a little short of 7 hours to complete all these tasks. Furthermore, let's assign 20 percent or 8 minutes padding to each task. The total padding would be 80 minutes, and these tasks would consume one entire workday of 8 hours without even allowing any time for breaks or lunch! What Parkinson's Law declares is that the additional 80 minutes would get consumed anyway, and when three of these tasks get delayed due to circumstances beyond our control it would take an additional 8 minutes! Now, let's create a dummy task called "Filler" and assign 24 minutes for its completion, and simultaneously take away the 80 minutes' padding from the 10 tasks.

On the schedule, the 11 tasks (10 plus "Filler") only occupy 7 hours and 4 minutes. If there is no need to draw upon the "Filler" buffer, the tasks will only take 400 minutes or 6 hours and 40 minutes. Even if three tasks get delayed as expected, the total time spent would be 424 minutes or 7 hours and 4 minutes. This will allow time for breaks and some lunch!

Parkinson's Law is related to procrastination and Student Syndrome (described later in this chapter). Procrastination is the tendency to put off into the future tasks due today. Student Syndrome has an upper limit to the delay (submission deadline) while procrastination *per se* is often open ended. Parkinson's Law differs from both in that it is not delaying the start of the task but the completion, that is, stretching the task to fit the time.

Let's compare this with getting a new bookshelf or kitchen cabinet. Within a few days, these storage locations get filled with all manner of things. Empty spaces and available time get filled with available things.

Murphy's Law

The premise in this law is very simple: if something can go wrong, it will. Unfortunately, things do go wrong at the worst possible moment, and where they can do the most damage.

There are two ways to look at this law: The first is a skeptical, cynical, pessimistic, or fatalistic view that merely leaves a sour taste in the mouth. The other is a view to cover all possible risk areas such that the predictable risk is surmountable with sufficient planning and redundancy. The objective in studying this law is to understand, predict or anticipate, and prepare for possible points of failure.

Murphy's Law does not work when you want it to, that is, it is not predictable nor can you rely upon something going wrong. The example is: it generally rains immediately after you wash your car, but if your lawn is dry and you wash your car hoping that it will rain and water your lawn, it won't.

The impact of Murphy's Law is that if it is not anticipated and planned for, it could be very disruptive. In projects and processes, there could be several simultaneous process paths, that is, several things could be happening at the same time. One of these paths would be considered critical, that is, the duration of the path would be the duration of the project as a whole. Disruptions on any other path would have almost no impact on the project but disruptions on the critical path will delay the project by a corresponding duration. Such is the impact of Murphy's Law on any project, process, or operation.

In the current context, deadline management, the impact of Murphy's Law is to make us miss deadlines.

As mentioned earlier, there are two ways of using Murphy's Law: as a problem or as a guide to finding solutions. It can be used as a planning tool, as we will see later in this chapter. Therefore, Murphy's Law is often regarded as a **principle of defensive design**.

The golden rule of planning states, "If you fail to plan, you plan to fail." A good plan considers points of failure and comes up with possible ways to address them.

This is relevant in time management, especially in the workplace, because unplanned emergencies waste time while situations that we have a solution for can be taken in our stride.

The following process can be used for the purpose of defensive design:

1. The first step is to identify points of failure. This is a two-stage method in which history ("What has failed in the past?") and speculation ("What could go wrong in the future?") are combined to come up with as large a list as possible. For example, while planning the kick-off meeting for a new project, we can take a look at what happened at the previous kick-off meeting (historic) and also see what else could happen (speculative). The last meeting may have been planned as an outdoors event and may have been rained out. One of the senior managers sponsoring or championing the project may have had to come from a different location and may have been delayed due to construction or traffic. The light refreshments ordered for the event may have been insufficient, arrived too late or someone may have been allergic to ingredients in the pastries. The PA system may have had technical difficulties, or the wire connecting the computer to the projector for the presentation may have been incompatible. Given what went wrong, we may be able to create a list of what else could go wrong. The points of failure would then include the weather, transportation, technology, hospitality, health restrictions, and so on.

2. For each point of failure, create a feasible solution. This step should involve as many minds as possible so as to brainstorm and feed off each other's knowledge and experiences.

3. In order to use this as a planning tool, use the possible points of failure to create contingency plans and alternative paths through the operation, that is, to create Plan B, Plan C, and so on. For example, in the kick-off meeting example detailed previously, Plan A would be to attempt to hold the event outdoors. Plan B, then, would be to erect a marquee to account for rain.

4. In order to use this as a defensive design tool, build in solutions to the points of failure right into the product such that the product not only does what it is supposed to do (positive traits), it also does not do what it is not supposed to do (non-negative traits). For example, in the same example as we covered previously, Plan A would include the marquee anyway for the refreshments. If it rains, the marquee would be expanded to include the people.

5. In order to find solutions to problems even before they occur, address points of failure identified but not experienced previously and create solutions for these problems.

My image of a point of failure is that of a chain whose strength depends on the strength of the weakest link.

The preceding five-step process strengthens the weak link.

Student's Syndrome

The Student's Syndrome is a tendency to delay starting an assignment until it is almost too late to get it done on time. For example, if a student were assigned a report to be handed in in two weeks, the typical student would not act upon it until the thirteenth day at which point he/she would put in a colossal effort and complete it in the nick of time.

The three issues of procrastination, Parkinson's Law, and Student's Syndrome are related. Procrastination is an open-ended delay or tendency to put off—the work may never get started or completed. Student's Syndrome is a tendency to delay but not open ended—the work gets done at the very last minute. Parkinson's Law generally does not indicate a delay in starting but the task does not get completed until the very last minute. The following table summarizes these issues:

	Parkinson's Law	Procrastination	Student's Syndrome
Start	Begins well	Delayed	Delayed
End	Just in time	May never	Just in time
Quality	Good	Unknown	Poor

The impact of procrastination is that the task may never get started, never get done, and the quality is unknown. Procrastination is an indicator of poor self-discipline and lack of interest in the outcome, although procrastination may sometimes result from fear of commitment, fear of failure, or even fear of success.

The impact of the Student's Syndrome is that the delay in getting started requires a tremendous effort to complete the task in time. This could lead to fatigue, stress, and other health issues. Moreover, in order to get the task completed in time, corners may have to be cut, which would lead to poor quality.

Popular legend claims that Roman Emperor Nero played the fiddle during the Great Fire of Rome in 64 AD. This is often used as a metaphor for doing something trivial at the time that a decision or action is required for a more pressing issue. Many people do work on trivial tasks and appear busy while more important tasks requiring attention remain undone.

As mentioned earlier, procrastination and Student's Syndrome could indicate:

> - **Lack of self-discipline**: Time that could be spent on the task is instead wasted in the pursuit of pleasures and self-indulgence.
> - **Lack of interest in the task**: There is no motivation to complete the task since there is no perceived value in the result of the action.
> - **Fear of commitment or involvement**: This is similar to why people do not voluntarily cooperate with the authorities in solving crimes. In the workplace, on-time completion of tasks could be taken to indicate affiliation with political factions within the organization, and delays could indicate non-involvement.
> - **Fear of failure**: Many people fear the stigma, notoriety, or derision they associate with failure.
> - **Fear of success**: People sometimes fear that success in a task would bring them more tasks of similar nature, something they would like to avoid.

The purpose of understanding the underlying causes of procrastination and Students' Syndrome is to recognize them when they occur, understand the trigger, and take steps to overcome it.

For example, if the underlying cause is lack of self-discipline, create accountability with a friend or peer and use a combination of rewards and punishment—the proverbial carrot and stick—to instil self-discipline. If the underlying cause is lack of interest, create motivation through a reward system. Fear of commitment or involvement can be reduced through encouragement and recognition. Fear of failure can be mitigated by working with the management to determine the limits of consequences of failure. Fear of success can be mitigated through a generous reward system.

Strategies

In the following sections, I will present two strategies to reduce the impact of Parkinson's Law, procrastination, and Students' Syndrome, and one strategy for reducing the impact of Murphy's Law. These strategies, when effectively used, will significantly improve time management skills.

Strategy 1 – Frontend load

Before introducing the concept of frontend load, let's see the reverse, backend load, which is a problem.

"Backend load" refers to little work on the task in the early part of assigned time followed by colossal effort at the last minute. What this means is that people have a tendency to put in only small amounts of work, if at all, in the initial time available for the task and then a huge effort in the tail end. This is because of an illusion, a trick the mind plays upon you.

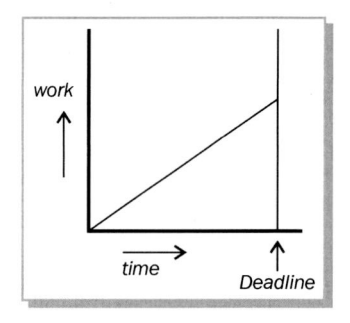

Even without considering external factors, there are three possible negative outcomes with backend load:

- **Overshooting the deadline**: Even a heroic effort at the last minute cannot sometimes get the work done in time.
- **Insufficient solution**: The alternative to overshooting the deadline is to compromise somewhere. One compromise is to deliver less. You could reduce the amount of work you do in order to get it in under the wire.
- **Low-quality solution**: The other alternative to overshooting the deadline is to compromise quality. You could reduce the quality of the work you do in order to get it done in time.

This approach, backend load, also leaves the task wide open to Murphy's Law. When more and more work is required to get the task done on time, stress levels go up. The scramble to complete the task makes a person fumble and make more errors. As a friend remarked very sagely, "The time to hurry is before we begin." Hurrying through a task almost begs errors.

One possible solution is what I call uniform load, that is, completing equal parts of the task in equal intervals of time. In mathematical terms, this may be stated as %t=%w, where %t is the fraction of time elapsed and %w is the fraction of work completed.

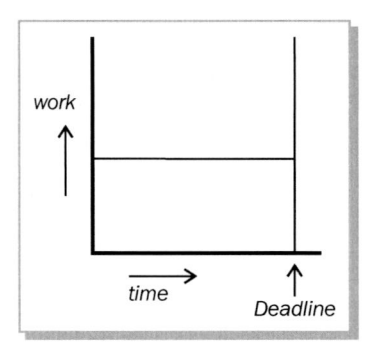

This is a possible solution to Parkinson's Law and a possible alternative to backend load. At least for planning purposes, this approach is highly recommended. A large task may be broken down into even divisions and assigned to even intervals of time.

There are three major problems with this approach:

> **Accuracy of estimate**: Is the time sufficient? An estimate is just that—an estimate. There is no guarantee that the task will indeed be done within the time. Therefore, even if the progress on the task were perfectly measurable, if the estimate is not accurate, the chances of missing the deadline still exist.

> **Measure of progress**: Is the task tangible? Can the extent of completion be accurately measured? Otherwise, there is no way of ensuring that the rate of tackling the task is indeed uniform. As one corollary to Murphy's Law reads, "95 percent of the project takes 5 percent of the time. The other 5 percent takes another 95 percent of the time!"

> **There is no protection from Murphy**. Even if the estimate is accurate and the progress can be accurately measured, uniform loading of tasks offers no protection from Murphy's Law. What if disaster strikes when you are 95 percent done?

The best alternative to backend load is to frontend the task. Frontend load refers to doing as much of the task as possible right up front.

This ensures that the solution is complete, of good quality, and even if the task is not tangible or if the estimate was not accurate, with most of the task done, the chances of hitting the estimate are very good.

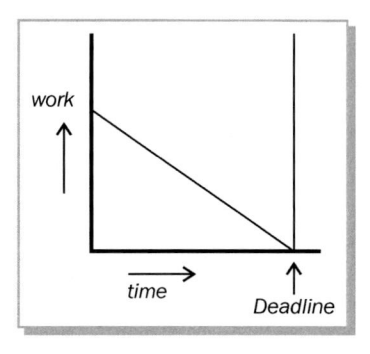

The focus of this technique is on two points:

> Address the largest, most significant, most complex, or riskiest part of the task first (risk includes the risk of delay).

> Time-slice units: Plan periodic targets. Setting these milestones will ensure that the task is proceeding as desired.

Frontend load has the following advantages:

- It reduces the probability of overshooting the deadline (it is still possible to overshoot the deadline if the estimate were inaccurate or if the scope suddenly increased).
- It does not require compromises such as reduced quality or sufficiency.
- This method provides some insulation against Murphy's Law.

Frontend load counters the limitation of uniform load by:

- Addressing the most significant part of the task first balances inaccuracies of estimation
- Use of the time-slice units ensures accurate measure of progress

---

Tip

Changing your perspective

When you see a mountain in the distance, it appears as small as a molehill, but when it is mere feet away, it is large. Similarly, when a deadline is far away in time, it is a mere molehill, but when it looms ahead, it appears as a mountain. The mind gives only as much attention to a task as its perceived size. When it is a molehill, the mind ignores it. As the task grows in size as the deadline draws nearer, the mind turns its attention upon it.

To overcome issues arising from this way of thinking, you can use what I call the *perspective strategy for efficiency*. If you were driving on a deserted highway and you notice a rock in the middle of the road about a mile away, you will not adjust your speed or direction until it looms near you. Similarly, when we look at a task along the time dimension, we will not react to the deadline until it looms large in front of us. People tend to look at tasks along the time dimension. To counter this, let us take a look at the task without any thought to the time available for its completion. Now, the task will grab our attention, we will see its true size, we will attack it, whittle it down to size, then overcome it.

Frontend load is a useful strategy for meeting deadlines especially with uncertainty and risk. By addressing the biggest, most difficult, and most uncertain parts of the tasks up front, possible points of failure are eliminated. This ensures smooth implementation.

The difference between a marathon and a sprint is that the marathon requires a steady effort over a long time and distance while the sprint requires a burst of energy over a short time and distance. A marathon can represent uniform load and a sprint the frontend load.

Strategy 2 – Artificial deadlines

When asked how long a task will take, many people overestimate on purpose. For example, someone may say, "I could probably analyze this data and give you a report in four days, but let me be safe and say that it will take me five days." This is called padding the estimate. We now know that it is a bad idea to pad estimates. For one, not every task needs a contingency buffer. For another, Parkinson's Law swells the task to consume the buffer such that when there really is a need for additional time, it is no longer there. This is the reason we create dummy tasks in the daily task list.

On the other hand, what if we tried to complete the task in less time? What if, in the example above, the person said, "I could probably give you a report in four days but let me try to do it in three days?"

An artificial deadline is an imaginary deadline whose purpose is to protect the true deadline. Even if the artificial deadline is not met, the chances of meeting the true deadline will be improved.

> **Make a note**
> Artificial deadlines do not mitigate Parkinson's Law.

The benefit of such a construct is to improve the probability of completing the task on time, that is, within the true deadline.

Imagine setting your watch ahead by 5 minutes in order to improve punctuality. Many people use this technique quite unsuccessfully. When we know that the watch is 5 minutes fast, we automatically subtract 5 minutes from the display. The practice of setting the watch ahead to ensure promptness can work only if the person concerned does not know that a) the watch is indeed fast and b) how many minutes ahead it is. Setting your watch forward works when you ignore what your mind is telling you!

My favorite story that drives home the concept of artificial targets is the wonderful achievement of the American athlete Jesse Owens in the 1936 Olympic Games. He achieved four gold medals at those games. The first gold medal was in the 100 meter sprint. The third was in the 200 meter dash and the final one was in the 4x100 meter relay.

Gold number two came in the long jump, where he fouled on his first two attempts. One was just a practice run where he continued down the runway into the pit, but German officials didn't buy it and counted it as a jump. Top German long jumper Luz Long suggested Owens play it safe and jump a few inches before the usual take-off spot. He took his advice and qualified for the finals, where he won the gold.

Even gold-medal winning Olympic athletes benefit from artificial deadlines.

How does this apply to the workplace?

Almost every task in corporate environments tends to be deadline driven. Artificial deadlines improve an employee's ability to meet and beat deadlines, and, therefore, to meet or exceed expectations.

Setting an artificial deadline for every task will soon defeat its purpose. Artificial deadlines should only be used for important and significant tasks. While artificial deadlines may be set at any arbitrary point before the true ones, the most effective artificial deadline point is about 80 percent of the true one. The Pareto principle seems to work very well here.

I refer to this strategy as the Jesse Owens Principle.

Strategy 3 – Failure management

In the previous two sections in this chapter, we addressed strategies for overcoming delays. In this section, we look at possible points of failure.

In the context of time management, identifying points of failure, avoiding them, and being able to recover from them ensures that we do not waste time when things do indeed go wrong. Precious time is wasted only if we are unprepared when crises occur.

In order to prepare for points of failure, we must address the following questions for each task:

> - What can go wrong?
> - In what way can things go wrong?
> - When can or will things go wrong?
> - How can we avoid points of failure?
> - How can we recover from failure?

Conceptually, all tasks will have the following points of failure:

> - **Process-related**: Incomplete process definition, obstacle to any step, incorrect sequence, dependencies, triggers, and so on
> - **Resource-related**: Wrong people assigned to the tasks, inexperience, apathy, unavailable resources, and so on
> - **External dependencies**: Tasks outsourced to external entities, waiting on parts, or tools required to complete the task, red tape, and son on
> - **Things beyond control**: Weather, health, personal emergencies

For each of these points of failure, we can list how they can go wrong, predict when they might go wrong, and identify prevention and recovery measures.

Experience is the best teacher. We do not have to experience failure directly in order to learn from it. Vicarious experiences work just as well.

There are two benefits we can glean from this process: we will be able to avoid most errors, and when some errors do occur, we will be able to recover from them quite quickly. We will not be able to anticipate all points of failure. However, when we run up against something new, we will be able to add a new entry to our list and will be able to avoid or recover easier the next time it occurs.

Many companies have a knowledge base of issues and possible solutions. The objective, therefore, is to start with a modest set of issues and solutions thereof, and to grow this set through experience.

Fire fighters do not wait for a fire in order to begin their planning and training process. They are effective at fighting fires because they anticipate and prepare for possible contingencies. Likewise, instead of waiting for things to fail in the workplace, anticipating, planning, and training for possible failures can prepare you for most situations.

One obvious application of this concept is in emergency planning. Emergency management agencies and local emergency planning commissions consider worst-case situations and plan for them.

Another application of this concept is in disaster recovery and business continuity planning.

Summary

This chapter introduced deadline management as the counterpoint to appointment or schedule management.

There are three major obstacles to meeting deadlines:

> Parkinson's Law or the tendency for work to expand so as to fill the time available for its completion
> Procrastination and Student's Syndrome, or the tendency to delay working on a task (procrastination is open ended, Student's Syndrome leads to a last-minute effort to get the task completed in time)
> Murphy's Law, or the tendency for things to go wrong

By addressing these obstacles, we have a greater probability of meeting deadlines.

We saw two strategies for combating Parkinson's Law and the delaying tendencies, and one to mitigate Murphy's Law.

The first strategy was frontend load or doing as much of the task as possible up front. The thrust is to get the most difficult, most critical, and riskiest parts of the tasks out of the way so as to smooth the way for the rest of the task.

The second strategy was to set artificial deadlines before the true deadline. Even if the artificial deadlines are missed, the odds of meeting the true deadlines are improved.

The third strategy was to identify possible points of failure and come up with solutions to avoid them and/or recover from them. Points of failure are problems only when caught unprepared. If we anticipate and prepare for points of failure, we can take them in our stride.

The next chapter introduces efficiency techniques. Peter Drucker defined effectiveness as doing the right thing, and efficiency as doing things right. Both are required for effective time management.

7

Overcoming Obstacles to Productivity

In this chapter, we will look at ways to complete tasks efficiently. Despite best intentions, many tasks do not get done on time if done at all. Peter Drucker defined **effectiveness** as *doing the right things* and **efficiency** as *doing things right*. Both are needed for a complete and comprehensive time management system.

In the previous chapters, we addressed *what* to do (task selection through prioritization and filtration) and *why* we do them (goals, intermediary objectives, and action plans). In this chapter, we will address *how* the tasks must be acted upon in order to complete them in the shortest time and with the least effort. In other words, **effectiveness** is a process for *task selection* and **efficiency** is a strategy for *task execution*: the former is used to manage tasks within the available time and the latter is used to manage time within the task. Effectiveness is a strategic objective; efficiency is achieved through the use of tactics.

Why do we need efficiency? On the one hand, it helps us meet our deadlines and time-bound obligations such that we gain a reputation for professionalism, punctuality, responsibility, and reliability. On the other hand, it helps us get more things done in less time such that we achieve more and also find the time to pursue our particular interests.

Obstacles

What are the typical obstacles that come in the way of getting work done efficiently? In the book *The Time Trap*, Alec MacKenzie identified 20 time wasters including:

- > Management by crisis
- > Telephone interruptions
- > Inadequate planning
- > Attempting too much
- > Drop-in visitors
- > Ineffective delegation
- > Personal disorganization
- > Lack of self-discipline

- Inability to say no
- Procrastination
- Meetings
- Paperwork
- Leaving tasks unfinished
- Inadequate staff
- Socializing
- Confused responsibility or authority
- Poor communication
- Inadequate controls and progress reports
- Incomplete information
- Travel

First, let's classify these problems. We can collect them at least under two groups, *internal* and *professional*.

Internal obstacles

Internal obstacles are personal habits and traits that come in the way of completing tasks. These obstacles relate both to personal and professional situations. These are issues that we have control over but some of these are very difficult to overcome:

- **Lack of self-discipline**: When there is no self-discipline, it is very easy to give in to temptation and to take the easy route. Self-discipline is the barrier that holds back other indulgences such as procrastination, distraction, and leaving tasks unfinished.
- **Procrastination**: The lure of procrastination is a combination of avoiding distasteful or less pleasing activities and seeking attractive or pleasing activities. Therefore, the less pleasing activity is put off until tomorrow while failing to acknowledge that tomorrow the temptation to procrastinate will be as strong. The solution is to look not at the activities and their relative attraction but at the consequences of doing or not doing the task.
- **Personal disorganization**: If the concept of "a place for everything and everything in its place" is not followed, much time will be wasted in constantly searching for things.
- **Attempting too much**: This is a clear indication of a lack of understanding of capability. As mentioned in *Chapter 5, Managing Daily Tasks*, an estimate takes into account the capability of the individual and the complexity of the task. The discipline of estimating the duration of every task will reduce the tendency to attempt too much.

- **Leaving tasks unfinished**: Like the problem of procrastination, this issue is the result of the focus on the action and not on the result. When the initial enthusiasm for the task wanes, the task becomes less interesting. Like the problem of procrastination, the solution is to focus not on the activities but on the results.

- **Inability to say no**: This can also contribute to why people take on more than they can reasonably hope to complete. It is caused by lack of courage, fear that refusing would lead to ostracism, or a general weakness of character that any strong personality could overwhelm and impose upon. The solution to this problem is to become unavailable, that is, changing location, being behind closed doors or not picking up the phone. If a person cannot be found, the question of saying yes or no is a moot point!

- **Socializing**: In today's environment, this includes use of social media (Facebook, LinkedIn, and so on). It is good to be social but not when there is work that remains to be done. Just as there must be a place for everything and everything in its place (refer to *Personal disorganization*), there must be a time for everything and everything in its time.

- **Inability to avoid telephone interruptions and drop-in visitors**. This relates to the previous two points. Being unavailable counters the inability to say "No" and excess socializing. The exception, of course, is that one should always be available for one's manager because the manager has a call on his or her staff's time, and a manager should be available for his or her people because, as Tom Peters explains in *In Search of Excellence*, a manager should support and facilitate the team so that the team can work excellently.

Professional obstacles

Professional obstacles are work-related issues. Most of these may be imposed by the work environment. We may not have direct control over or the ability to correct them. We have to work around them. A few of the obstacles are given here:

- **Inadequate planning**: While it is true that things do not always go according to plan, it is no reason not to plan carefully. Adages, chestnuts if you will, like "A minute spent in planning saves ten in implementation" and "If you fail to plan, you plan to fail" are indeed true. Many obstacles to implementation are the result of poor planning.

- **Ineffective delegation**: The best delegation is when we delegate our weaknesses to other people's strengths and thereafter refrain from getting involved. Delegating a task to someone who is not strong in that area leads to poor implementation and getting involved negates the delegation to the point of creating the micromanager from hell.

- **Inadequate staff**: If the management does not provide enough people to complete the tasks that must be done within the allocated time, it forces the existing staff to take on more than they can reasonably hope to achieve before the deadline. While this may not be changed, it is best to bring this to the management's attention so as to set the right expectations.

- **Incomplete information**: While it is sometimes required to get started without knowing everything about the task at hand, information is required at some point in time in order to proceed. Just as poor organization leads to time wasted in searching for things, incomplete information leads to time wasted either in searching for information or in undoing thing done wrong.

- **Inadequate controls and progress reports**: If the management does not properly steer the team based on the latest status information, much time will be wasted later in course correction. Frequent and accurate status information will lead to the right checks and balances.

- **Confused responsibility or authority**: The armed forces use the concept of the "chain of command" to ensure that orders flow only in one direction. If a person receives conflicting commands from multiple levels in his or her chain of command, it could lead to wasted effort and rework. Therefore, even if you have indirect authority over someone, allow commands to flow strictly through the chain of direct authority.

- **Meetings**: Not all meetings are productive for all concerned. When invited to a meeting, it is important to ensure that the agenda is relevant before accepting or attending it. If people attend meetings that they have no business to be in, their time is wasted.

- **Paperwork**: While paperwork such as status reports and time tracking is important, some forms that are passed around to fill out are unproductive. Questioning the relevance of the paperwork asked for could lead to greater productivity.

- **Travel**: In this day and age of virtual meetings, travel can be justified only when face-to-face meetings can truly make a difference.

Here is my own set of 10 things people do that are not in the least productive. I have broken this set down into three groups: emotion, thought, and action. In each of these items, I have included the words of wisdom from one or more experts in various fields. As Sir Isaac Newton observed, "I have seen far because I have stood on the shoulders of giants."

Emotion

Sometimes it is not what is done but how and why that makes a difference. Emotions contribute to both aspects.

Emotions in general, particularly negative emotions such as anger, fear, and jealousy, take your attention away from the task at hand. If your mind is not on what you are doing, you will take longer to do it. Anger relates to things that occurred in the past and a fear (worry) of things yet to come. On the one hand, this may be a character trait: some people find things to worry about! On the other hand, this may indicate that there is no task on hand that occupies the person's attention enough. It is good to think about the future, to have dreams, visions, plans, and goals, but not good to spend much time and thought on it. Likewise, the past is what makes us who we are, so it is good to think about it, learn from it, and take some pleasure in it, but not good to dwell upon it. You cannot do anything about the past except come to terms with it.

Marcus Aurelius said, "*Remember that man's life lies all within this present, as 't were but a hair's-breadth of time; as for the rest, the past is gone, the future yet unseen.*"

Franklin Delano Roosevelt was famous for the words, "*There is nothing to fear but fear itself.*" Why worry about things we have no control over? We must plan to mitigate what could be and resign ourselves to what comes. Worrying is an absolute waste of time. Control your emotions and get more done quickly.

Thought issues

Thoughts also contribute to how and why tasks are performed in a certain manner. Also, thinking of other than the task at hand, that is, lack of focus, could slow down the implementation and lead to poor quality.

> **Thought inertia**: After a heated discussion, have you found yourself thinking "I should have said this" or "I wish I had said that?" The French call this l'espirit d'escalier, the spirit of the staircase. Your mind is lingering over the last task even as you move on to the next task. This inertia is due to the emotion that went into the task—the more you get attached to your task, the greater the inertia.
> The trick, therefore, is to distance yourself from a task when it is complete.
> As Tennyson wrote, "The old order changeth, yielding place to new."

> **Indecision**: Results are produced by actions, and decisions trigger actions.
> If, as in Shakespeare's Hamlet, "To be or not to be" is the question, any action before the question is answered is premature. Johann Wolfgang von Goethe said, "Then indecision brings its own delays, And days are lost lamenting o'er lost days." Sometimes it is the fear of making the wrong decision that causes the indecision. Other times, one may hide behind indecision as the reason not to take action. Once the decision is out, action cannot be avoided. Indecision is a procrastinator's refuge. Problem solving and decision-making is as much a time management skill as organization, prioritization, planning, and execution.

> **Not thinking things through**: Every solution breeds problems. Actions have consequences, and the consequences of actions must be identified and evaluated before deciding upon the course of actions. The great management guru Peter Drucker said, "The future is not going to be made tomorrow; it is being made today by the decisions and actions we take with respect to the tasks of today." By this, today's problems are the results of yesterday's decisions and actions, and if we only move from problem solving to problem solving, we are moving into the future backwards! We can avoid this cascade of problems by thinking things through. Actions not only have primary consequences but, according to Dr. Peter Senge, they may have secondary, tertiary, and other consequences due to the systems effect. Thinking things through can mitigate most systems effects.

> **Insufficient separation of thought and action**: The Yankee baseball legend Yogi Berra once remarked, "How can you hit and think at the same time?" In other words, you cannot think and act at the same time because the thinking gets in the way of the doing and the doing gets in the way of the thinking. If the action requires your focus, you cannot let your thoughts wander, and if you do act while thinking of something else, your actions will be prone to errors. The best approach is to think first and act afterwards.

> **Lack of predetermined response to possible situations**: Do you have a plan B? Plan C? Plan Z? When things do not go as planned, if we don't have a backup plan, we react. It is not possible to think things through when we react. On the other hand, if we have considered possible scenarios and thought about what we would do if they occurred, we don't react but respond. James Yorke said, "The most successful people are those who are good at Plan B."

Action issues

While thoughts and emotions affect what is being done, only actions produce results. It is important to do the right thing at the right time in the right manner and for the right reasons.

> **Do-overs**: Many people believe in the saying, "There is never time to do it right the first time, but there is always time to do it again." However, when you do a task wrong the first time and get to attempt it again, time is a-wasting! Henry Wadsworth Longfellow wrote, "It takes less time to do a thing right, than it does to explain why you did it wrong." Peter Drucker said, "Efficiency is doing things right; effectiveness is doing the right things." I would add that there is greater efficiency in doing things right the first time. I accept that there could be circumstances wherein it is necessary to cut corners, but such should be the exception than the norm. A good friend of mine once told me, "The time to hurry is before you begin." By being well prepared, thinking things through, and performing the task with discipline and focus, errors and the need to do things over can be reduced. Metrics play a large part here—by keeping track of your errors, you can find ways of reducing them.

> **Unused wait time**: Waiting is a fact of life. We wait in queues at post offices, banks, airports, supermarkets, train stations, bus stops, doctors' surgeries, and so on. There are things we could be doing in this time. At the least, there may be some reading to catch up with. At the most, work that lives in the "pending" column could be put paid to. Benjamin Franklin said, "Dost thou love life? Then do not squander time, for that is the stuff life is made of." If you don't put wait time to good use, you are, in effect, squandering time.

> **Parking on a task (tinkering)**: Some people cannot leave a completed task well alone. They re-open the task to tweak it. And tweak it. And tweak it. The task takes a very long time to be put to rest. And in the meantime, other tasks suffer. Bente Borsum said, "Art knows no limit, and the artists will never achieve perfection." Economists know about the law of diminishing marginal utility—in this case, the value of each tweak is successively less, perhaps exponentially, and does not justify the time spent upon it. Avoiding tinkering calls for discipline but can be achieved through the use of incentives (even self-imposed) that encourage the expeditious completion of any task and disincentives that discourage delays.

> **Poor recovery from interruptions**: Interruptions are a part of life. Much as we would like to avoid being interrupted while focusing upon a task, we cannot ignore all calls on our time. Life is not polite. It does not stand by waiting for us to complete one task before throwing the next at us. Natural disasters, business, and personal emergencies claim the right to interrupt us. Interruption, too, is a choice. When an interruption beckons, we can evaluate it against our values and priorities and decide whether or not to be interrupted. There are two problems with interruptions: first, after the interruption has been taken care of, we need to be able to resume what we were doing prior to being interrupted; and secondly, we need to recognize that interruptions may themselves be interrupted. If we cannot recover from the interruption, the task we started may never get done. American racecar driver Mario Andretti said, "Circumstances may cause interruptions and delays, but never lose sight of your goal."

When we are aware of these obstacles to productivity and efficiency, we can recognize them when they appear. The importance of knowing about them is to avoid them when possible, recognize them when they appear, and recover from them when we realize that we have fallen into their clutches. For example, when we receive commands from both the manager and the manager's manager, we must recognize the problem as "confused authority and responsibility" and bring it to the manager's attention immediately. It is then the manager's responsibility to re-establish the chain of command and avoid conflicting authority. Likewise, the tendency to "park on a task" must be recognized and the task should be brought to closure so as to move on to the next task.

Preparation

Many, if not most, tasks can be completed more efficiently with a little preparation. Contrast these two approaches to the same task: putting together a desk.

Andy tears open the carton and dumps all the pieces out. He does not believe in reading the manual; the preparation time was 2 minutes.

Andy picks up the topmost pieces in the pile and tries to put them together. These are not compatible—they depend on other pieces. Andy then searches in the pile for the pieces they depend on, tries to figure them out, and finally takes out the manual after wasting 15 minutes. The first step according to the manual involves attaching rubber floor protectors to the bottom surface of the pieces that would form the sides of the desk. Andy walks over to the garage and searches in a pile of tools for a hammer—a waste of another 15 minutes. Andy finally finds the hammer, goes back, and knocks in the rubber floor protectors. The next step is to lay the back of the desk flat on the floor and attach the sides using screws and a flat-head screwdriver. He rummages through the pile of pieces to get to the back. When Andy tries to put the back of the desk down, he realizes that there is not enough room to build the desk right there. He moves the pile of pieces and spends about eight minutes stacking them better to make room. He goes back to the garage to search for the flat-head screwdriver. Ten minutes later, he finds it and goes back to building the desk. Step three involves attaching the top with Philips-head screwdriver—back to the garage, the pile of tools, and another ten-minute search. After the top is attached, the other pieces—the frame for the shelf and the trimmings—take only a couple of minutes more. With all the interruptions, putting the desk together takes Andy a little more than an hour.

Betty first makes sure she has enough space to work in. She opens the box, takes out the parts, and stacks them on one side. She then reads the manual and determines that she needs one flat-head screwdriver, one Philips-head screwdriver, and a small hammer. She gets these tools from the tool-chest and keeps them accessible. Based on the order of operations in the manual, Betty restacks the pieces so that she can reach the next piece when she needs it. The preparation time for this is 10 minutes. Betty hammers in the rubber floor protectors to the bottom of the side panels with the nails provided, lays the back panel flat on the ground and then screws the two side panels to the back with the screws provided and the flat-head screwdriver. She sets the piece upright and attaches the top panel with the screws provided and the Philips-head screwdriver. She attaches the frame for the shelf with a flat-head screwdriver and finishes trimmings with the Philips-head one. The implementation was 15 minutes and total time spent was 25 minutes.

Lack of preparation is one of the biggest wasters of time. Preparation results in a smoother implementation.

Related to being prepared is being organized. In the previous examples, Betty had a place for everything and everything in its place, while Andy had to search for every single thing. When you know where something is expected to be, you can save a lot of search time. Being organized per se is a great time saving device.

In general, you need to prepare:

> **The place (location and space)**: Is this the right location to accomplish the task? Which is the best location to work on the task? How much space do I need? Do I have enough space? Preparing the place for the task includes identifying the location and ensuring that the space is sufficient and ready.

> **The pieces**: Do you have all the materials, tools, data, recipe, ingredients, and so on, required for the task? Preparing the pieces for the task includes identifying and collecting everything required for the task.

> **The people**: Are other people involved in this task? It's necessary to identify and gather the people involved in the task.

Crisis management

While "managing by crisis" is one of Alec MacKenzie's top time wasters, it is still necessary to know how to manage a crisis. The knowledge reduces the time it would otherwise take to respond to the crisis.

What constitutes a crisis? It is a problem that needs *immediate* resolution. Under ordinary conditions (that is, when time is not the critical resource), there are many processes that may be used to solve the problem. However, all of these processes consume considerable amounts of time and may not be suitable during crises.

A crisis is disruptive because it upsets the planned and expected order of operations and actions. There is a tendency to freeze up and shut down. The strategy to managing crises is to have a well-defined process for addressing unexpected problems, that is, to have a good problem-solving methodology.

I put forth two different processes for solving problems.

The first is the "standard" process to use under ideal conditions. This process takes time but finds the best solution for the problem. By taking the time to think things through, possible holes and negative consequences may be identified and avoided. I call this the "best fit" process, the process to find the best-fit solution. The steps are:

1. Understand the problem through information gathering and analysis.
2. Create possible solutions through brainstorming (no judgment, look at everything objectively).
3. Identify a set of criteria to evaluate the candidate solutions.
4. Evaluate and rank the solutions.
5. Pick the best solution.
6. Implement the solution.

During a crisis, however, it is not possible to take the time to think things through. I compare this to how emergency medical professionals handle patients. They solve the immediate problems, stabilize the patients, and call in the specialists to drill down to the root causes. They do not perform brain surgery in the ER but do ensure that the patient is alive and available for the surgeon to do their job in the OR. In other words, problems are solved twice. I call this the "first fit" process wherein the objective is to stop looking for a solution as soon as one that fits the immediate need is identified. The steps are:

1. Understand the immediate problem—where is the fire? Where is the bleed?
2. Define the minimum that must be done to fix the immediate problem—put out the fire, and stem the bleed

3. Until a solution is accepted:
    1. Create a solution.
    2. Evaluate it to see whether it fits the immediate problem.
    3. Accept or reject.
4. Implement the solution but plan to revisit the problem so that it does not create future problems.

Interruption management

Interruptions are inevitable. They are the biggest obstacles to keeping to schedules and completing tasks on time. Interruptions disrupt the normal flow of thoughts and actions, and negate carefully laid plans, timelines, and preparations. If unchecked, interruptions can cause tasks to be left incomplete, reduce quality and attention to detail, and ultimately reduce the amount of spare time available for recreation and enjoyment.

Life is not polite. It does not wait until you have completed the task at hand before it throws another task at you.

When an interruption occurs, you can choose to ignore it or to handle it. For example, the caller ID on the phone allows you to determine whether you want to take that call or let it go to voicemail.

How do you decide whether or not you will let yourself be interrupted? What will make you take away your focus from the task you are working on in order to handle the interruption?

It is almost the same choice you make when you determine what the best use of your time is. Just as you rank the tasks on your list according to your goals and values in order to pick your next task, you evaluate the interrupting task and see whether it has a higher priority than the task you are working on.

The first thing to understand is that only *urgent* tasks can be interruptions. Something that is not urgent will not clamor for your attention. The second point is that for something to take your attention away from whatever you are working, it must be *more important* than the task that you are currently working on.

Therefore, when an interruption occurs, that is, when there is an urgent request for your attention, evaluate the threat. If it is not important, ignore it, that is, delete it from the realm of possible things you could do. If it is important, check to whether it is indeed more important than the task on hand. If it is, accept the interruption.

There is another factor to consider: can this interruption be delegated to someone else or are you the only one who can take care of it. In other words, how important are you to the task that has slipped past the "importance" filter?

Sometimes, it is difficult to distance yourself from any task. Ego and emotions can get in the way of such decisions. Try to put this in perspective: stress is the result of giving something more importance than it deserves. If you think that you are more important to the task than you really are, you cannot let go and distance yourself from the task. This will lead to stress, especially when you cannot stop what you are doing in order to take care of the interruption.

The first part of managing interruptions is to avoid being interrupted. If you decide to let something interrupt you, you should then control the interruption.

If you do choose to get interrupted, you must ensure that the task that you had been working on gets your attention as soon as the interruption is done. The ability to pick up from where you left off reduces the disruptive effect of interruptions. However, it is still not without loss. The mind cannot switch contexts in a blink of the eye. Interruptions do reduce productivity and efficiency. We have no choice but to live with them and make the best of our abilities.

Have you ever been in a moving vehicle when it made a sudden start or stop? Or, how about getting on or off a moving vehicle? In either case, your body takes a little time to get used to the sudden change of momentum. Without the time to get used to the sudden change in momentum, or without something to hold on to when such sudden changes occur, you will lose your balance and fall over. This is a demonstration of Newton's first law of motion—"Every body at rest or in uniform rectilinear motion remains at rest or in uniform rectilinear motion unless acted on by an external force". This law is otherwise known as the law of inertia.

The mind is not very different. It works by associations. The phrase "train of thought" is very accurate—it follows a track, most often a track it has followed through before, and moves with a high momentum. Switching the mind from one track of thought to another requires slowing down this train and moving to the other track. When the train of thought gets forcibly switched by an abrupt interruption, it even gets derailed. The more disparate the thoughts (and trains) are, the greater the effort it takes to switch from thought to thought. If switching thoughts take so much effort, how about switching tasks that take thought?

Self-discipline

Lack of self-discipline is identified as one of the top time wasters, especially as a personal obstacle. What exactly does this mean? Self-discipline is that part of personal mastery that prevents or controls yielding to the pleasurable trap of temptation and indulgence. This is particularly an issue when it leads lower productivity and poor quality.

For example, it is tempting to play just one game of FreeCell or Solitaire just to take a break, reduce stress and think better when you return to work. The questions to ask yourself are:

> - Do you *really* need a break? Didn't you just take a break ten minutes ago? A five-minute break every hour is "acceptable."
> - Can you stop after just one game? Won't you be tempted to play just one more? And one more? And one more?
> - Will this game really reduce your stress and help you think better? Or is it just an excuse to indulge in a pleasurable activity?

Lack of self-discipline takes away precious time from the task at hand. Many people substitute one indulgence for another. For example, people who try to quit smoking take up chewing gum. Substitution does not always work, especially if the indulgence is deeply ingrained.

There is no true solution for lack of self-discipline. What I have found is that as long as it is not recognized as an issue (that is, denial), there cannot even exist a plan for its solution. The solution, when it comes, must come from within and cannot be imposed from an external source.

Here is a suggestion: just as some people look to achieve their goals by asking someone they trust to be a coach who imposes accountability, self-discipline can be inculcated by including tai chi, meditation, yoga, and so on, as group activities. It can be started with the express purpose of improving focus, concentration, and mental prowess.

Taking responsibility

When things go wrong, the easiest thing to do is to blame someone or something else. For example, you may hear someone say, "I followed the instructions perfectly. I am sure the machine is flawed." This tendency leads to the practice of finding a scapegoat to take the fall for failures.

What is the long-term result of such a behavioral trait? Would you trust a person who blames external entities for failures? How far would such a person get in life, or how high could such a person climb the corporate ladder? What would such behavior do to the person's conscience?

Taking responsibility is not easy. It takes courage and strength of character. It requires sacrifice and may often have negative consequences. However, it has many positives. It builds a person's reputation and respect. People look up to those who take responsibility. Such a person would be given greater responsibilities and move up rapidly in the corporate ladder.

Blaming others is not productive. It does not yield results. It merely avoids consequences—for a time. At some point in time, consequences catch up with such behavior.

Successful people are responsible for their actions and the consequences thereof. They stand behind their work. They get results. They are productive and effective.

Deliberate distractions

After working intensely for hours on a grueling task, do you feel inclined to respond to the first thing that clamors for your attention, no matter how unimportant?

Some tasks are long, laborious, and monotonous such that one actually welcomes a modicum of distraction. Also, just as any voluntary muscle, the human brain gets fatigued by intense application especially when the task is boring and interest lies elsewhere. A break eases this fatigue. According to Nathaniel Kleitman, the human brain works best with a 20-minute break after 90 minutes of work. Others like Dr. Ernest Rossi have noted the 90-minute cycles, with peak focus for about 45 minutes. Tony Schwartz of the Energy Project recommends three 90-minute sessions in 8 hours of work. The verdict is out—don't work for more than 90 minutes at a time on any task.

What if you do go beyond the 90-minute recommendation? Two things happen. First, your productivity drops sharply. Second, you are a sitting target for the next distraction that waits around the corner.

Let's say that you are working on a report expected to take about 4 hours to complete. After you work on it for about 90 minutes, your focus will wane enough for you to be susceptible to interruptions. At this stage, if you wait for nature to take its course and send you the first distraction that comes its way, you may end up with something that you don't really want to do and you wouldn't allow yourself to be interrupted by under better conditions. However, because you are tired of the task at hand, you may end up with such an interruption.

What is the alternative? The alternative is to deliberately distract yourself. Here is how it works:

1. Make a list of short tasks (10-15 minutes). This is the "deliberate distractions" list.
2. Set a timer for 75 minutes
3. After the timer signals you, bring the main task to a logical pause, that is, a safe state to be interrupted. Make a note of all the things that would enable you to resume the task easily.
4. Take a 20-minute break.
5. Complete one of the tasks on your list of deliberate distractions.
6. Restart the 75-minute timer and resume the main task.

This is a very powerful tool to control brain fatigue.

Exercises

The first exercise in this chapter is a discussion to identify time wasters not listed in earlier sections. This discussion serves to extend the list and also to make the students aware of and be alert for potential time traps.

The second exercise in this chapter is to identify one occasion in your lives when you did not meet a deadline, identify reason(s) why things took longer than assigned or estimated, discover how you could have recognized the time trap(s), and come up with strategies to avoid the time trap(s) or recover from it (them) when it (they) occur(s).

The third exercise is an on-going activity—to keep track of time wasters and devise strategies for avoidance and recovery.

Summary

Effectiveness and efficiency are complementary concepts both of which are required for a comprehensive view of time management. In the chapters so far, we have explored effectiveness. This chapter gave us an overview of efficiency. This chapter only covered a few efficiency tactics. It is beyond the scope of this book to cover efficiency in greater depth.

The first concept is to avoid the usual time wasters. These are the normal obstacles to productivity and efficiency. The chapter lists 30 such obstacles. The second concept is to be efficient through organization and preparedness. By bringing together the right people and necessary materials to the right place, and by acquiring required information, the action will flow better. The third concept is to manage unexpected problems by solving the immediate problem and buying time to find the best solution.

The fourth concept is to avoid or management interruptions. Interruptions are inevitable but their impact does not have to be inevitable. The fifth concept covered in this chapter is the concept of improving productivity by deliberately taking time away from the task at hand. As counterintuitive as this may seem, this is a very powerful technique to avoid brain fatigue.

The next chapter introduces metrics. Peter Drucker said, "If you can't measure it, you can't manage it." Time management is no exception to this rule. The next chapter offers several ways to measure how well we manage time. The metrics help identify areas in which we are doing well and areas in which we need to improve. Tracking these metrics over time can show how we are improving—or not improving—our time management skills.

8
Measuring Your Time Management Skills

In this chapter, we will look into practical ways to measure time management skills and track the metrics over time to evaluate progress over time.

Peter Drucker said, "If you cannot measure it, you cannot manage it." Therefore, in order to *manage* time, there must be an appropriate measurement system. In particular, there must be an *objective* method to track use of time. This chapter covers metrics for productivity, effectiveness, efficiency, punctuality, and on-time completion of tasks.

Why measure?

Here are 10 reasons why even a seemingly innocuous activity such as time management must be supported with a good measurement system:

1. **Metrics provide insight**: Metrics such as productivity and efficiency are not mere data points or facts. By evaluating and analyzing these metrics, it is possible to identify strengths and weaknesses.

2. **Metrics set expectations**: For example, historic values for productivity and efficiency measures set the standard for *future* productivity and efficiency. They can help *predict* and track use of time.

3. **Metrics allow budgeting:** Complementing the previous point about expectations, metrics not only set expectations but also set *limits*. For example, the expectation that a task would take two hours would allow you to set aside that amount of time, that is, budget the time, when planning for the task.

4. **Metrics aid in planning**: For example, knowing how much time is available for tasks and knowing how long each task will take will determine how many tasks can be completed in the available time and how the other tasks must be disposed of (delegate, defer, and delete).

5. **Metrics promote objective decision-making**: For example, when trying to decide which of two activities has a higher priority, unless there was a way to *compare* the relative merit or value of the two activities, any decision would be arbitrary and subjective.

6. **Metrics justify decisions and actions**: Complementing the previous point of objectivism in decision-making, past decisions, and actions may be justified based on the measurements that supported them and the results that they produced. For example, if the choice of one task over another competing task was ever questioned, metrics that formed the basis for the choice may be presented.

7. **Metrics motivate**: For example, if metrics were used to evaluate the employees' *performance* and *compensation*, they may be used to motivate and reward.

8. **Metrics support accountability:** When employees know that their performance will be evaluated according to certain measurements, they will diligently keep track of and report the same measurements. In this context, metrics can be used to set goals and to navigate towards the goals. Indeed, the "M" in SMART goals stands for "measurable".

9. **Metrics identify improvement:** For example, if a task took an hour in the past, repetition would hone skills such that the task would get done in about 50 minutes. However, if there were no metrics, the improvement would not be recognized. Likewise, metrics identify areas that could do with improvement, that is, areas of poor performance.

10. **Metrics improve learning:** For example, by setting goals, tracking, evaluating, and motivating through the use of metrics, there is an association between the metric and the behavior. This promotes better understanding and learning.

Metrics also boost self-image and confidence in one's own ability. They allow you to take pride in your achievement.

The ultimate purpose of measurement is to manage, in keeping with Peter Drucker's statement.

What should be measured?

There are those who collect many measurements and analyze the data in order to understand the past. There are many time management dashboards with multiple metrics and measurements that track the use of time to the smallest detail. Any dashboard is not effective if it does not *improve* time management skills. It is better that we measure in order to take action for the future and to improve results.

Towards this goal, there are four sets of metrics covered in this chapter. The first set measures productivity and effectiveness. The second set indicates punctuality. The third set shows organization and control. The last set shows efficiency. The rest of the chapter shows how these metrics must be collected and used.

Here are the four metrics sets:

1. Metrics Set 1 (Productivity and Effectiveness):

    - **Productivity Index**: This is the average number of tasks you complete per unit time. For example, if you complete 8 tasks the first day, 7 tasks the second day, 10 tasks the third day, and only 4 tasks the fourth day, your productivity index is 8 tasks per day. To be useful, the tasks must have about the same complexity or be expected to take the same amount of time. If the tasks are expected to take very different amounts of time, *Productivity Index* may be calculated using a weighted average explained later in this chapter.

    - **Effectiveness Ratio**: This is the ratio of achieved results to expected results. For example, if you expected to achieve 10 tasks in a day but only completed 8 tasks, your *Effectiveness Ratio* is 80 percent. To be useful, your expectation must be reasonable.

    - **Quality**: There are two ways of measuring poor quality—omissions, that is, how many right things did you not do, and errors, that is, how many wrong things did you do? *Quality* may be measured in an absolute sense of total mistakes (errors and omissions) over a unit of time or in a relative sense of mistakes per unit of work.

    - **Depth of incoming tasks**: This is the maximum number of unanticipated tasks that get queued up. As tasks get completed, new, unanticipated tasks continue to arrive and get queued up. The depth of the queue indicates how quickly the queue gets acted upon and disposed. It is an indirect indicator of effectiveness.

2. Metrics Set 2 (Punctuality):

    - **On-time Arrival**: This is the ratio of the number of times you arrived on time to a scheduled meeting to the total number of meetings you attended within a reference period expressed as a percentage. For example, if you attended 50 meetings in a month and arrived at all but 4 of them on time, your On-time Arrival for the month is 92 percent. On the other hand, if you only arrived at 22 meetings on time, your *On-time Arrival* is only 40 percent.

    - **On-time Completion**: This is the ratio of the number of deadlines you met to the total number of deadlines faced within a reference period expressed as a percentage. For example, if you faced four major deadlines in a month and met or exceeded three of them, your *On-time Completion* for the month is 75 percent.

3. Metrics Set 3 (Organization and Control):

    - **Unanticipated Tasks**: This is the ratio of unanticipated tasks to total number of tasks, expressed as a percentage. A well-planned and organized day has few surprises. A low value of unanticipated tasks indicates a high degree of planning, organization, and control.

4. Metrics Set 4 (Efficiency):
   - **Time Saved**: This is the difference between the estimated and actual duration of a task. For example, if a task is expected to take an hour but only takes 50 minutes, the *Time Saved* is 10 minutes. Time saved can be accumulated over periods of time and compared.
   - **Effort Efficiency**: This is the ratio between expected and actual task duration expressed as a percentage. For example, if a task is expected to take an hour and is completed in 50 minutes, *Effort Efficiency* for the task is 120 percent.

Collecting metrics

Collecting metrics should not become so cumbersome an activity that it gets dropped altogether. Towards that end, the nine metrics described previously require very few pieces of data and can be collected as a matter of habit rather than an additional effort.

To begin with, all tasks must be assigned an estimate, that is, an expectation as to how long the task will take, and all meetings and appointments must be assigned a **definite start time (Mtg)**.

As a task is started, the **start time (S)** must be noted. As the task is completed, the **finish time (F)** must be noted. If a task is interrupted, the duration of the interruption must be noted and subtracted from the total time taken for the task. *Actual duration = F-S less interruption.*

As a meeting or appointment is joined, the **arrival time (Avl)** must be noted.

As new tasks come up, they must be added to the "super" list. If these tasks are of sufficient urgency to be disposed of right away, they must be added to the current day's list and marked as unanticipated. They then contribute to the depth and unanticipated tasks statistics.

One point to note here is the concept of **normalization** used to determine Productivity Index and Effectiveness. In order to compare tasks, there must be a common basis. For example, David Allen in his book *Getting Things Done* recommends that a task should be about two minutes long: anything longer should be broken down into sub-units and treated as a project. I submit that two minutes may be too short a time, and that a quarter of an hour may be a workable unit of work at least to start with. Therefore, for purposes of capturing productivity and effectiveness metrics, a task should be treated as a set of units of work each a quarter of an hour long.

The nine metrics can then be calculated thus:

- Productivity Index = # equal tasks completed / day. If the tasks are very different in expected duration, they must first be normalized.
- Effectiveness = # equal tasks completed / # equal tasks in the list. If the tasks are not equal, they must be normalized.
- Quality measures must be gathered after the tasks are completed and checked for errors, that is, quality is a product of the action but an attribute of the result. Relevant numbers are average number of mistakes per day and both total and average number of mistake per task. Mistakes include both errors, that is, wrong things that were done, and omissions, that is, right things that were not done.
- Depth of incoming tasks= max # unanticipated tasks in queue.
- On-Time Arrival = [# times Avl < Mtg] / Total number of meetings.
- On-Time Completion = # tasks deadlines met / # total deadlines.
- Unanticipated Tasks = # unanticipated tasks / # total tasks completed.
- Time Saved = Total Estimated Time – Total Actual Time Taken.
- Effort Efficiency = Total Estimated Time / Total Actual Time Taken.

Using the metrics

The purpose of collecting metrics is not merely to understand the past or sit on one's laurels but to learn, take suitable actions and bring about the future. The question, therefore, is obvious: how do we use the metrics? How do we improve ourselves with these metrics?

The first step is to take stock as to where we stand. The path to any destination can only be determined with reference to a starting point, that is, if anyone asks "How do I get to your location?", the counter question should be, "Where are you coming from?" When we know how productive, effective, efficient, punctual and dependable we are (or not), we can determine which traits we need to change or improve, set targets to meet and take steps to bring about the change or improvement.

Dr. Eliyahu Goldratt created a three-step change process. The steps involve answering the questions:

1. What should you change?
2. What should it be changed to?
3. How can you bring about the change?

Using the metrics described earlier, the previous steps may be used to improve every area of time management. Let's now see how the process may be used so as to become more productive, effective, efficient, punctual, dependable, and to produce better quality work.

How to be more productive

In this section, we use the Goldratt three-step change process and relevant metrics to improve productivity.

1. What should you change?

    The relevant metric is the Productivity Index. Normalized Productivity Index measures productivity in terms of uniform units of work per day. This means that improving productivity requires increasing the number of uniform units of work performed. For example, let's use a uniform unit of work that is 20 minutes long. Considering an eight-hour workday, Productivity Index can have a maximum value of 24, that is, 24 units of work per day. This is almost impossible to achieve due to meetings, interruptions, disruptions, distractions, and context switching (that is, the time it takes to change your thoughts from one task to another). Nevertheless, a low value of Productivity Index is a clear indicator that productivity is insufficient and must be improved.

2. What should it be changed to?

    This step involves determining a target value for Productivity Index that is high enough and yet can be attained, that is, to determine a realistic value for Productivity Index and set that as a goal to achieve. Again, such goals must be SMART.

3. How can you bring about the change?

    Parkinson's Law, procrastination, interruptions, distractions, and so on, are obstacles to productivity. If you can monitor your time and reduce waste, you can increase the PI metric. One way of pulling out of attractive but unproductive distractions is to set an alarm to get your attention every 15 minutes (work unit).

How to be more effective

In this section, we use the Goldratt three-step change process and relevant metrics to improve effectiveness.

1. What should you change?

    The implication of this metric is to be able to achieve everything planned for the day. There are two ways to achieve this: complete more tasks or plan for fewer tasks. While this may appear to be poor advice, the true implication of this is to strive for "realistic" daily task lists. The maximum achievable Effectiveness Ratio is 100 percent. Even if you complete all the tasks on the daily task list and take on unplanned activities, the ratio cannot exceed 100 percent. Is 100 percent achievable? Yes, if the list is strictly kept to what can be reasonably done in the time available. A low value of Effectiveness Ratio is a clear indicator that effectiveness must be improved.

2. What should it be changed to?

    Effectiveness Ratio of 100 percent is achievable and must be set as the target.

3. How should you bring about the change?

    The keys to achieving Effectiveness Ratio of 100 percent are to keep the tasks on the daily list under control and not take on unplanned activities until the planned activities are finished.

    This may not be totally under your control: the task that you must work on may be set by your manager's priority and not by your own.

How to be more efficient

In this section, we use the Goldratt three-step change process and relevant metrics to improve efficiency.

1. What should you change?

    Effort Efficiency (EE) is the ratio of the estimate to the actual time to complete the task (expressed as a percentage). If the actual time exceeds the estimate, Effort Efficiency will be less than 100 percent. If the estimate exceeds actual time, Effort Efficiency will be greater than 100 percent. It is possible to consistently complete tasks in less time than estimated and thus consistently score more than 100 percent on this metric. The efficiency metric compares the actual time taken for a task with the estimate. An estimate, as discussed earlier, should reflect the complexity of the task and the capability of the individual performing the task. EE, therefore, compares capability (potential) against effort (realization of the potential). At the time of implementing the task, the estimate should already be on record. The only variable left is effort. An EE value that is consistently less than 100 percent is a clear indicator that efficiency is insufficient and must be improved.

2. What should it be changed to?

    If Effort Efficiency is consistently less than 100 percent, the target Effort Efficiency has to be set to 100 percent or better.

3. How should you bring about the change?

    There are two parts to changing the efficiency metric. If Effort Efficiency is found to be less than 100 percent, the two ways to improve this are to revise estimates and to increase effort. The efficiency techniques mentioned in the chapter on managing deadlines may be used to reduce time taken on tasks and thus improve Effort Efficiency.

How to be more punctual

In this section, we use the Goldratt three-step change process and relevant metrics to improve punctuality.

1. What should you change?

    How important is it to be on time to appointments and meetings? In some corporate cultures, a little delay is acceptable as long as it is not a regular feature and can be explained. On the other hand, there are many establishments where punctuality is very critical. A punctuality metric that is less than 100 percent is a clear indication that punctuality is insufficient and must be improved.

2. What should it be changed to?

    The target On-Time Arrival must be set to 100 percent. The corporate culture must determine the acceptable margin of tardiness.

3. How should you bring about the change?

    While the concept of artificial deadlines has been explained in the context of deadline management, it is equally applicable in management of punctuality. To cure chronic lateness, set artificial meeting times.

How to be more dependable

In this section, we use the Goldratt three-step change process and relevant metrics to improve your dependability.

1. What should you change?

    Dependability is usually associated with reliability and trustworthiness. People associate this trait with on-time task completion. For example, the common expression is, "You can count on (depend on) him or her to come through in time." On-Time Completion is the primary metric for dependability. If this metric is less than 100 percent, it is a clear indicator of insufficient dependability and must be improved.

2. What should it be changed to?

    The target On-Time Completion must be set to 100 percent.

3. How should you bring about the change?

    There are two points in dependability that you must keep in mind: there is an external entity involved, that is, someone is depending upon you for something; what you do and how you do it determine when you will be done. When an external entity is involved, perception is reality. Therefore, it is enough to do what it takes to be perceived to be dependable. What this means is that the best approach to improve the dependability metric is to complete the broad strokes early and fill in the details afterwards. By doing so, the progress is tangible and appreciable.

How to improve quality

In this section, we use the Goldratt three-step change process and relevant metrics to improve quality.

1. What should you change?

    There is no true measure of absolute quality. Perfection has no metrics. There are two relative quality measures: errors and omissions. Errors refer to the presence of negative actions or results. Omissions refer to the absence of certain positive actions or results. Lots of mistakes, that is, mistakes in excess of acceptable limits, are a clear indicator of poor quality and must be improved.

2. What should it be changed to?

    Perfection implies zero mistakes. The objective, therefore, is to minimize mistakes and strive towards perfection.

3. How should you bring about the change?

    From a purely implementation point of view, errors are the result of not thinking things through, that is, haste in thought, and omissions are the results of not checking on work done, that is, haste in action. The obvious process for minimizing errors is to avoid haste in thought or action. If haste cannot be avoided, that is, if there is insufficient time or if there is a crisis, apply the "emergency room" formula: act on the twice, once to solve the immediate symptom and once to solve the underlying problem.

Summary

This chapter covered four major points. The first section was a justification of the use of metrics especially in the area of time management. This section listed the ten major purposes for the use of metrics.

The second point was an enumeration of metrics applicable to time management. These were classified under productivity and effectiveness, punctuality, organization and control, and efficiency. The metrics are:

1. Metrics Set 1 (Productivity and Effectiveness):
    - Productivity Index
    - Effectiveness
    - Quality
    - Depth of Incoming Tasks

2. Metrics Set 2 (Punctuality):
    - On-time Arrival
    - On-time Completion

3. Metrics Set 3 (Organization and Control):
   - Unanticipated Tasks
4. Metrics Set 4 (Efficiency):
   - Time Saved
   - Effort Efficiency

The third point was a list of data items that must be logged in order to calculate the previous metrics. The final point was about using the metrics to improve productivity, effectiveness, efficiency, punctuality, dependability, and quality.

In the next chapter, we will see the use of tools such as task lists and planners in time management. Traditional time management used paper products but the modern world has many electronic tools to get the same results.

9
Tools

In this chapter, we will discover the different tools that can help us manage time, from simple lists to calendars, organizers, alarms and reminders, and journals. A tool is just that—a tool. The value of a tool is in its effective use. This chapter covers how these tools may be leveraged to make the best use of time.

Earl Nightingale said, "No one can manage time. I only manage activities." In this book, we have seen that time management is the management of activities, appointments, and deadlines. In this chapter, we will see how tools can help us manage these aspects of time management.

From an orthogonal point of view, time management can be broken down into four process areas:

- Planning
- Remembering
- Executing
- Evaluating

The value of each of these areas cannot be stressed enough. There is no point in planning something if you fail to remember to execute the plan, and since paper—and, in these days, electronic aids—remembers what the mind forgets, tools play a large part in remembering. In this chapter, we will ensure that the various available tools help us in these areas. In particular, we will look at processes that take tasks, appointments, and deadlines and use tools such as lists, calendars, alarms, and logs to plan, remind, facilitate (implementation), and evaluate (metrics). This creates a system both for use of the tools and for continuous improvement.

Tasks

At the simplest level, a to-do list is merely a list of tasks that we either think of doing or that some external entity (person, incoming e-mail, thought association, and so on) requires of us. The list is best created in the order in which these thoughts or triggers occur, but it does not follow that they must be handled in the same order.

For example, consider the following list:

- Pay bills
- Call cable company re: credit for outage
- Pick up pants from laundry
- Order cake for Aunt Sally's surprise party
- Make appointment to have car serviced

Most organizers and planning diaries have places to create task lists, and most personal computers, laptops, and smart phones have provisions for to-do lists. Notepads and index cards may also be used to maintain to-do lists.

The process for managing tasks

Let's now see how to follow the process of planning, remembering, executing, and evaluating in managing tasks:

- **Planning**: As mentioned earlier, we may add to the list in the order in which the tasks are "triggered". The next step is to prioritize the tasks (urgency/importance or ABC/123) and delete or delegate the lower priority tasks and defer the tasks that are not urgent. We can then estimate how much time each task should take. Finally, the best way to ensure that the remaining tasks get done is to make an appointment with the tasks, that is, fit the tasks into gaps in your appointment calendar (discussed later in this chapter). I recommend the use of two lists:
    - A **master** list that is used to record tasks as they come into existence
    - A **daily** list that is the output of the prioritization (ABC/123), filtration (delete, delegate), and assignment (fit to time available for tasks today)
- **Remembering**: The task list must always be accessible such that when we have some time, for example, due to a gap in our appointment schedule, we can start working on the next available task. We can also set reminders including a string around a finger; an alarm on a watch, phone, or computer; a pop-up reminder on a computer; and so on to keep the task list constantly at the peak of our awareness.
- **Executing**: There are three parts to implementing a task: preparation, thought, and action. Preparation can take place any time before actually working on the tasks. Thought must precede action, and, like preparation, can occur any time before the action. Execution, in this context, refers to the action involved in implementing the task. When we have the time, for example, between appointments or while waiting for external input, take the next task on the list and begin working on it. Completing the task takes something more than just available time—it takes focus, determination, diligence, or, in a word, discipline. Any observations relating to the task must be captured in a journal (described in the section on calendars later).

> **Evaluating**: The first step to evaluation is to note what happened, how it happened, and any thoughts related to what happened—in other words, keep a journal. How long did the task take? Was the actual time close to the estimate or was it way off? Did things go as planned? What could be done better? What went well or better than expected? Can it be repeated? Were there many interruptions or distractions? Making relevant notes and learning from experience ensures better results the next time.

Appointments and meetings

As mentioned in *Chapter 4, Schedule Management*, all meetings and appointments have common characteristics including purpose, people, location, date, and time; that is, why, who, where, and when. These must be tracked on calendars or planners/organizers to ensure that the time slots are blocked. When the entries are made on the calendar, it helps us find available time and to avoid clashes, that is, to avoid scheduling two events at the same time.

Make a note

Curiously, the existence of the appointment or meeting addresses the *What?* question, that is, the question "What is a meeting or appointment?" leads to the answer "A meeting or appointment is a scheduled encounter between relevant individuals at a specified place and time for a specific purpose." Many meetings and appointments also result in coming up with how something may be resolved. Thus, appointments and meetings address all the six questions, what, why, who, where, when, and how.

Paper products

Just as tasks get recorded in lists, appointments and meetings should get recorded in calendars or planning organizers. Until the early 1990s, before the advent of technology such as PDAs (personal digital assistants) and desktop-based schedule managers such as Lotus Notes and Microsoft Outlook, most people managed their schedules on paper products. All of these products manage tasks (to-do lists) and appointments. These paper products are still very popular, although smart phones and web-based products have now become the most widely used schedule management tools. I have included examples of two typical paper products, the Day-Timer daily planner and the Franklin Covey two-pages-per-day sheets. (These companies also have weekly and monthly planners. I prefer the daily planner especially for new entrants to time management. The daily pages enforce discipline.) These are among the most popular of the available paper scheduling tools.

Tools

Day-Timer

Day-Timer (http://www.daytimer.com) is one of the oldest brands of planners and organizers. This is a very traditional layout now used by many planners.

The Day-Timer planner has a few lines for appointments and scheduled events, an area for tasks (action list), an area for recording expenses, and a space for keeping track of work done. The expense record is useful for keeping track of and getting reimbursed for work-related expenses. The work tracker is useful for people who bill their time to their clients and have to track their time to a high level of detail. These two items, the expense record and detailed track of billable time, make the Day-Timer the ideal tool for business travelers, sales people, and lawyers.

Franklin Covey planner

The Franklin Covey planner (`http://franklinplanner.fcorgp.com/store/`) is one of the most popular brands of planners and organizers. While the content is similar to the Day-Timer planner or any generic planner, it is very conducive for use with Franklin Covey's notation for tracking task status.

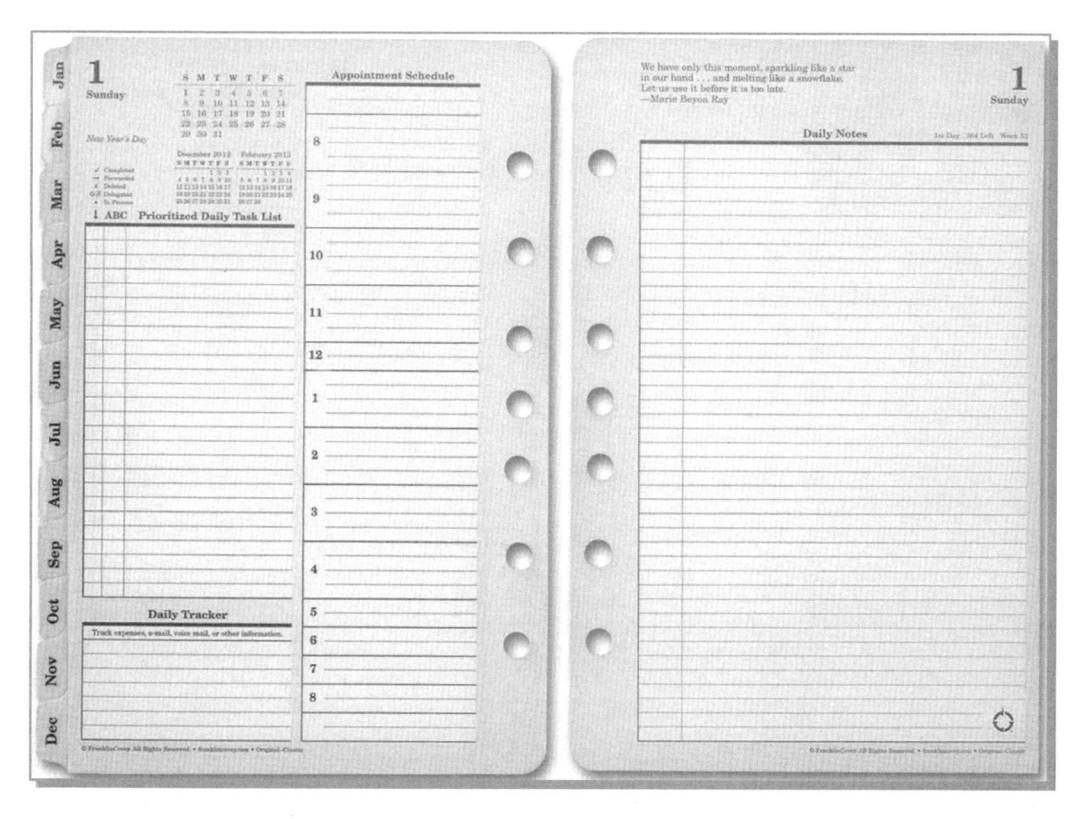

The Franklin Covey daily sheet has an hour-by-hour planning section; a very elaborate task list; a generic tracker for expenses, e-mails, voice mail, or other information; and a daily notes session to keep track of work done or merely record thoughts. The status of every task can be recorded with symbols denoting complete, forwarded (to the next day), deleted, delegated, or in progress. My only comment on this mechanism is that my own preference lies in delegating or deleting tasks even before they get to this list. This planner is very generic and can be used by everyone. It is particularly useful for people whose day is very orderly and predictable.

Technology

Every desktop operating system, every tablet, and every smart device today has some form of schedule tracking and task tracking software. The advantage in separating the task tracking from schedule tracking is that the incomplete tasks do not have to be copied over from one day's to-do list to the next. The major advantage one gets from using electronic products for schedule management is the ability to automatically set reminders for every event. Every electronic product also has a built-in clock such that reminders can be set to intrude upon our senses. Intrusive alarms and reminders ensure that we close the current activity or meeting in order to get to the next meeting on time. PDAs such as the Palm and HP's iPaq used to allow synchronization between their calendars and desktop calendars via cradles connected to the desktop. Modern smart phones synchronize automatically without the need for physical connections.

The following screenshots from Outlook and Google calendars show activities listed. Both these systems allow calendars to be shared and to invite attendees to events. These reduce the complexity of the logistics of creating appointments and meetings. The ability to add color focuses our attention to activity categories immediately. Both give the user the ability to view events at different levels of granularity—daily, weekly, and monthly. This allows for different planning horizons and adjusts to different levels of demand.

Outlook calendar

The Microsoft Outlook calendar is very suitable for collaboration and meeting management. In addition to the common features described previously, it allows resources (for example, conference rooms) to be reserved online. With web access through OWA (Outlook Web Access), the calendar can be viewed from any web connected device from anywhere in the world!

Google calendar

The Google calendar has a very useful feature in addition to the common features mentioned previously. It is a web application to start with, and the online version synchronizes automatically to the Android tablet or smart phone versions.

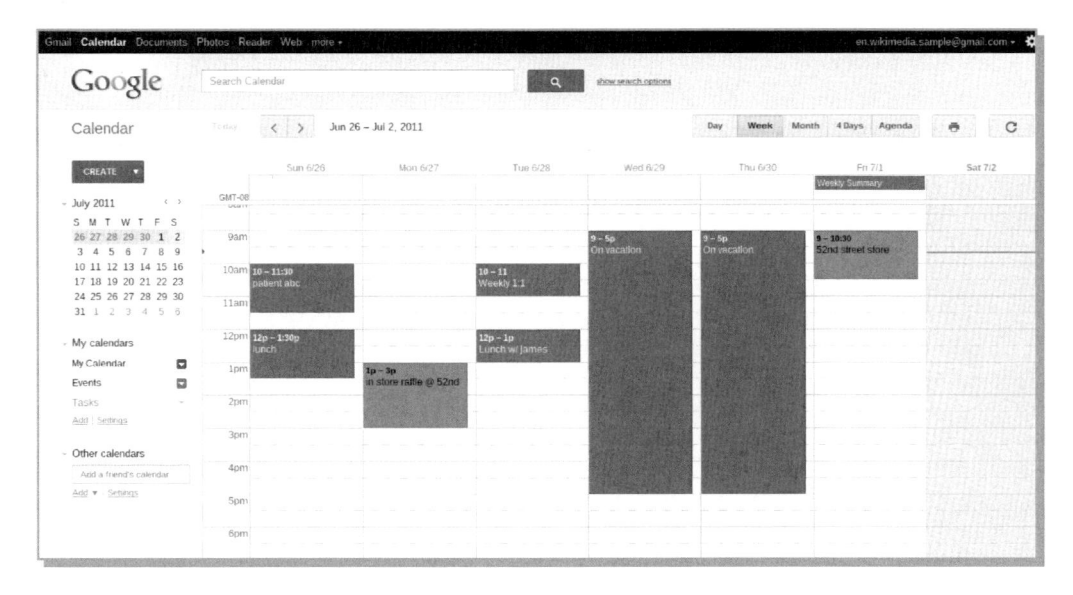

In all of the preceding tools, there are areas in which we can make notes and capture our thoughts. It is important to keep some kind of a journal in order to understand and improve what we do and how we do it—keep what works and reject what does not.

The process for managing appointments

Let's now see how to follow the process of planning, remembering, executing, and evaluating in managing appointments and meetings:

> **Planning**: The first part of making appointments is to determine whether the meeting is relevant, appropriate, and essential for us to attend. If we originate the request, that is, we create the event, identify attendees and location, and send out the invitations, the questions are moot. On the other hand, if we receive the request from someone else, the questions determine whether we accept or reject the invitation. The next part of making the appointment is to determine whether the time slot is available or not. If the time slot is available, including the time it may take to travel to the meeting and return to the next meeting, if any, the appointment can be added to the calendar with no problem. If the time slot is not available, the two options are to make the slot available by either canceling or moving whatever occupies the time or to request a different time and/or location for the meeting. Finally, when it is determined that the meeting is acceptable and the time slot is open, the meeting must be added to the calendar using any of the paper or electronic products described previously. Planning also involves setting alarms/reminders and setting up tasks to prepare for the meeting.

> **Remembering**: When setting reminders to ensure that we arrive at the meeting on time, it is important to note that the alarm or pop-up note may intrude upon a task in progress. I suggest setting up two alarms—the "true" alarm to get moving towards the meeting, which is set to go off with as much time as it takes to get there in time for the meeting, and a second alarm earlier than the "true" alarm to allow the task at hand to be done or left at a logical break point.

> **Executing**: There are three parts to execution with regard to meetings: leaving for the meeting with everything required and with time to spare, attending the meeting, and capturing meeting minutes. Appropriate reminders and alarms will ensure we leave for the appointment in time and with everything we need. When we attend the meeting, we must make sure that the agenda is followed especially with regard to the items of interest to us. If we are responsible for taking and disseminating the minutes of the meeting, we should be taking appropriate notes. The "meeting minutes" template from the previous chapter on meetings should be used. In particular, we should note the discussion and disposition of agenda items, issues and resolutions, follow up actions, who actions are assigned to, timeframes, and escalation procedures. Any other observations must be captured in a journal.

> **Evaluating**: The relevant questions to ask when evaluating meetings are: Did it start and end on time? Did the right people attend the meeting? Was there an appropriate agenda? Was the agenda followed? Was there a proper process to discuss and resolve all items on the agenda?

Deadlines

Deadlines are the limits before which time-bound tasks must be completed. Many tasks may be "urgent", that is, the results of the tasks may be desired or required immediately or as soon as possible. Deadlines, on the other hand, have hard stops. While the task may be completed any time before the deadline, the task may not go beyond the deadline without consequences.

Deadlines are very useful in that they force results. "Urgent" tasks demand attention and even action but do not necessarily get the right results, especially if there is no time to think things through and find the best solution. With "urgent" tasks, the first solution is usually a temporary one that compromises quality for speed. Deadlines, however, while time-bound, usually allow enough time for a good solution to be formulated and implemented. Deadlines allow one to focus and work faster and effectively.

The process for managing deadlines

Let's now see how to follow the process of planning, remembering, executing, and evaluating in managing deadlines:

- **Planning**: The first thing to do while planning around deadlines is to identify time-bound tasks and flag them as such. The deadlines may be externally imposed, for example, proposal submission, filing forms at government agencies, and so on; contractual, for example, service level agreement, guaranteed uptime, and so on; or self-imposed, for example, quotas. A task that has been identified as time-bound should be tagged with additional information such as the nature of the deadline, time limit, how hard the deadline is (that is, is it a "hard" or inflexible deadline or a "soft" or flexible deadline), and an indication of the value of meeting the deadline or the cost of failing to meet the deadline. Finally, after identifying the time-bound task and noting its characteristics, the task must be scheduled almost as though it were an appointment in order to ensure completion in a timely manner, including noting the "appointment with the task" on the paper or electronic calendar of choice.
- **Remembering**: Just as we set reminders and alarms in the calendar tool of choice to be punctual and prepared for all meetings and appointments, doing the same for deadlines will ensure that we complete time-bound tasks as expected. Just as we give ourselves two reminders for appointments so as to complete the task at hand and leave for the appointment with ample time, we should use the same concept to be able to leave the task at hand and complete the time-bound task.
- **Executing**: Time pressure affects different people in different ways. Some people thrive under pressure while others freeze up. Deadlines do cause anxiety and stress. It is important to keep the deadline in perspective and work towards it without letting anxiety get the upper hand. The tactics for managing deadlines (*Chapter 6, Deadline Management*) will come in handy in the execution phase of this process. Any observations must be captured in a journal.
- **Evaluating**: Since every individual is unique, it is important to understand what works and what does not work when it comes to handling deadlines. One process cannot fit everyone, especially since each person reacts in a different manner to deadlines, pressure, stress, and anxiety. Therefore, the purpose of taking notes and evaluating the process is to put together the process that works for us—for you and for me—in the best possible manner.

Summary

This chapter covers the process of planning, remembering, executing, and evaluating three kinds of activities—tasks, meetings, and deadlines—using tools such as task lists, planners/organizers, and journals.

It is important to note that the tools merely serve to implement and support the process, that is, to focus on the tool is to wag the dog. In other words, the process may be followed without tools. However, the process is much easier to follow when we use the tools.

Time managements systems are not only about planning to execute; they are also about remembering to do so. To plan tasks is simply to decide when we want to perform tasks and to describe them beforehand. Time management is about the will and awareness to execute tasks based on a plan, and this chapter provides the tools and ideas for both planning and performing tasks.

Made in the USA
Middletown, DE
17 October 2018